I WAS **BROKE** NOW I'M **NOT!**

HOW MY FAMILY WON WITH MONEY

D0170464

JOSEPH SANGL

"Now I'm Not" Publishing

This book is written to provide accurate information on the subject matter covered. Please be advised that Joseph Sangl is not engaged in rending legal, financial, accounting, tax, or any other professional advice. Before making any decisions regarding your own personal financial situation, you should first seek the advice of a proven and competent professional.

Printed in the United States of America by Morris Publishing – www.morrispublishing.com

Cover design by Ken Wilson – www.avclub.us

Library of Congress Control Number: 2007909081

Sangl, Joseph

ISBN 978-1-60530-190-7

First Edition

To my bride, Jennifer.

She is THE REASON that we are
winning with money today!

I love you!

ACKNOWLEDGEMENTS

I have always heard people say things like "I couldn't have done it without your help!"

That is the absolute truth in the case of this book. This book is the result of the time and effort of many.

I want to thank my parents, Roy and Sandra Sangl for teaching me the value of work and the power of compound interest.

I want to thank my five brothers – Greg, Jeff, Mike, Keith, and John for not beating me up too often and for all being entrepreneurs with "CAN-DO" attitudes!

I want to thank my friend and pastor, Perry Noble, for providing me an opportunity to launch this crusade at NewSpring Church.

To NewSpring Church and Staff, thousands of lives have been changed as a result of your commitment to Jesus Christ! Thank you!

Paul Marshall, you are a very wise man. Thank you for wisdom!

Sam and Lori Schmucker, you guys were there at the start of the crusade and have absolutely modeled the way of sound financial management! Thanks for being such great friends and leaders!

Mike and Traci Yoder, you helped Jenn and I wrestle with the decision to launch this crusade for years! Thanks!

Dave Ramsey, you provided the words and book at the right time in my life and as a result, I have been able to go do exactly what I was put on earth to do! Thank you!

Acknowledgements

David Chilton, your book, *The Wealthy Barber*, taught me the power of compound interest at the age of twelve. My life was changed because of that lesson!

Parker-Hannifin [NYSE: PH] Doug VanLue, Mikeal Brown, Ben Sprague, John Kashmer, Bill Noë, Ed Kent, Chuck Dydasco, Len Barnes, Bruce Rice, Brian Adams, Angie Crabill, Bob Schaefer, Steve Barnes, Kurt Keller, and Rob Howe – You guys rock! Note to the PH ESD GMT - You guys endured four years of Sangl yelling about money and were so supportive when I made the difficult decision to exit Corporate America to embark on this crusade full-time. I will never forget the going-away party! By the way, I have never used the "For Use In Case Of Extreme Emergency" envelope!

Jennifer Barden for helping edit this book. Thank you!

To those who have allowed me to look at your entire financial picture – your trust in me blows me away! Your stories of life-change are what inspire me to do what I do!

And to my best friend and bride – Jenn – words can't sum up what you mean to me! You are the best counsel I could ever seek. I could not have embarked on this crusade without your help and encouragement. I love you!

My daughter, Melea. I love watching you grow up, and I pray that this book helps set the example for you that a good life is found when you are doing exactly what you have been put on this earth to do!

CONTENTS

FOREWORD

Joe Sangl is an absolute freak—which is exactly why you should not just read, but devour this book.

As a pastor I have seen hundreds of people walk around carrying regret with them. What kind of regret? Well, there's relational regret—and then there's vocational regret—but the one that usually isn't mentioned but is probably most common is FINANCIAL regret. I know way too many people who are in debt up to their eyeballs and are currently seeing no light at the end of the tunnel—thus leaving them feeling hopeless.

But there is hope! If you are in a financial hole you CAN get out of it...and...if you are just beginning your financial journey in life what you are about to read can save you from making dumb money decisions that could haunt you for years and prevent you from doing exactly what God has designed you to do.

I personally believe that God has a unique plan and purpose for everyone on this big ball of dirt we call earth. However, I have seen people that, because of intense financial bondage, have to delay what they know He has called them to do because "they can not afford to make that move." That is tragic!

Let me be very clear about something—what you will read in the pages that follow is NOT "how to get rich in a month" type of thing. AND—by reading this you will not discover some obscure verse in the Bible that, upon "claiming" it you will have something to force God to bless you with.

What Joe has written about here is how the "average" person who makes an "average" salary can live an "above average" life. I am sick and tired of people who say that if they just made more money then they could get out of the financial prison they are in—that is BULL! You can begin your journey to freedom today, but remember, financial freedom takes work...

Which is exactly why many people never achieve it! I have met WAY too many Christians who simply want God to pay off all their financial debt—which is unfair because He's not the one who racked up the credit cards. God will help us get out of debt—but we have to be the ones who apply the wisdom He provides us with.

Let me be honest—this is not a very comforting book when you first read it. In fact, I sort of had a sick feeling in my stomach because of some steps I discovered that I need to take. BUT—I can promise that if you read and apply what has been written here then you will eliminate financial regret from your life.

On a personal note—I have watched Joe and his lovely bride walk through this journey. I have listened to him yell at the television when credit card commercials come on. I have seen him pay cash for just about everything he purchases…in other words—he is smoking what he is selling. This book is not the words of some ghost writer or some guy that has an abstract theory—but rather a guy who has been buried in financial regret, came out of it and wants to help others do the same.

— Perry Noble

Perry Noble is the founding pastor of NewSpring Church in Anderson, SC.

PREFACE

"If you had one million dollars, what would you do?"

My friend Tim asked me this over lunch one afternoon. I paused mid-bite of some delicious refried beans and rice to consider his question. For the first time in my life, I really thought about the real point of this question: "What have you been put on this earth to do?"

I had little idea of the influence this question would come to have on my life.

The year was 1999, and I was having lunch with Tim, a fellow engineer, at Los Hermanos in Clemson, South Carolina. It was a typical ordinary day. Just lunch. Just friendly conversation. Just time for a break from work. Just time for a life-changing question.

"If you had one million dollars, what would you do?"

What a question! I thought about it, but I could not give Tim an answer. I <u>did</u> <u>know</u> that if I had a million dollars, I *would not* be doing what I was doing then, but I had no clue what I would do.

"If you had one million dollars, what would you do?"

This question messed me up! I thought about it the rest of the day. When I went home that evening, I told my wife, Jenn, about Tim's question. I told her that I really could not come up with a good answer.

"What?!!!" Jenn exclaimed! "You couldn't even think of some vacations we could take?!"

"That's not the point of the question," I replied. "The point of the question is NOT what temporary things you would do. The point is what would you do for your life's work? What have you been put on this earth to do?"

From that very day, I began a search for exactly what I have been put on this earth to do. That one thing I have been created to do. That one thing that wells up a passion in me like no other. That one thing that makes me wake up every single day and say, "Yes!!! I get to go to work!!!"

This book is about the very thing that I have been put on this earth to do.

My life's passion statement is "To help others accomplish far more than they ever thought possible."

Helping others with their personal finances is my life's work. I have not invented anything in this book. I have put together information that I believe is foundational to financial success.

Jenn and I have applied these principles and tools to our lives and achieved financial freedom. If you APPLY the principles and tools taught in this book, you too will be able to win financially!

1 Introduction

I met Jenn at college. It was my first weekend as a freshman at Purdue University in West Lafayette, Indiana. I was committed to keeping my education first and foremost in my life. However, after meeting Jenn the first week of school I tossed my education focus out the window.

Even without a laser-like focus on my education, I did manage to graduate with a Bachelor of Science Degree in Mechanical Engineering, and I even did it in four years. I learned a lot about heat and mass transfer, thermodynamics, statics, and dynamics. I learned a lot about ESPN, friendships, other cultures, and living without accountability to anyone. I learned a lot about how to earn money, but I did not learn *anything* about what to do with that money once I got it.

Digging a financial hole ...
How did I pay for college? Loans, of course. I had taken loans from my father for the first two years and for the final two years, my friend Sallie Mae took care of me with Stafford Loans. I did work during the summers and managed to pay for about one semester's tuition and all of my books with cash, but I let Sallie Mae take care of the rest.

After four years of vacation ... uh, I mean, college, I was handed my engineering degree. I started my first full-time engineering job the day after I graduated.

Now, work ethic has never been a problem for me. But money management? Well, that is another story!

Chapter 1 – Introduction

I was earning a great salary as a beginning engineer, but what do you think I did with the money I earned? That's right! I spent all of it – plus some more.

Jenn had decided to obtain some additional classes and this required her to attend Purdue for one additional year. We were engaged for that year and our wedding date was set for about a month after her graduation.

Now, I had been working for a year, and I knew that her car needed replacing. I took the fact that it had been sitting broken down and abandoned in a Purdue residence hall parking lot for six months as a good sign that it needed to be replaced. I thought that it would be really cool to buy her a brand new car for her graduation. So that is exactly what I did. I had no savings, so I bought her a new car with 105% financing. I even financed the sales tax! I am sure that I paid full retail price (and then some) for that car. I made that salesman's quarter! Maybe even his year!

I will say that it was really cool to see Jenn as she unwrapped her graduation present. I remember her pulling out some of the gifts from the box I had given her and getting to the bottom to find a Purdue University license plate holder. I then reached out and handed her the keys. It was a very cool moment. She was pumped! I was pumped as well, but I also knew how much debt I had just signed us up for!

A few weeks later, we were married! Off we went to Jamaica for the honeymoon, much of it financed with debt. We needed appliances for our unfurnished apartment, so we purchased all of them with 100% debt. I needed a truck, so I bought a used one from my dad with no money down.

Chapter 1 – Introduction

I had purchased quite a few things on credit cards during college and this spending habit did not end after graduation. I could always make the monthly payments, but somehow the debt just managed to continue accumulating on the accounts. Advanta – my first credit card. The GM Card – another card. MBNA, Capital One, American Express, and the list goes on …

Anyway, here is a summary of all of the debt we (mostly me!) brought into our brand new marriage:
- Credit Cards
- New Car
- Used Truck
- Appliances
- Dad's College Loans (Mine)
- Sallie Mae Student Loans (Mine)
- Sallie Mae Student Loans (Hers)

They say that the number one thing that married couples fight about is money, so this is just what our new marriage needed – a pile of debt to manage.

We were horrible at short-term savings! We spent everything we brought home, plus some. How did we spend more than we brought home? Debt! We piled up the debt on our credit cards.

Our money management techniques were weird! I would have $200 deducted from every single paycheck and placed into a savings account. This was a great concept, BUT I would move that $200 from the savings account into the checking account every single payday! Why? I had to have it to pay the bills!

Each time I was paid, we entered an interesting balancing act because we would have to figure out which paycheck was paying which bills. If there was an unplanned expense like a car repair, it was not good! We would scramble to pay the bills and then let the credit card companies pick up the rest. Ugh!

Well, nine months after we were married, we transferred from central Indiana to Anderson, South Carolina. We were now living in a place where we literally knew no one. I highly recommend that couples do this at least once in their life! It was a great time of learning who each other was and strengthening our commitment to our marriage. But in keeping with our tradition, it was also time to acquire more debt. So we purchased our first home.

By some miracle, we managed to scrape together a 5% down payment for a conventional mortgage to buy our first house. So now our debt listing had a new member. This one was different than the others – it had SIX figures! Yikes!

We chose not to change our spending behavior so the debt continued to build. The checking and savings account balances continued to hover right at $4.13! The chart shows our bank account balances at the end of each month. SCARY!

Savings Account Balances (BEFORE Debt Freedom!)

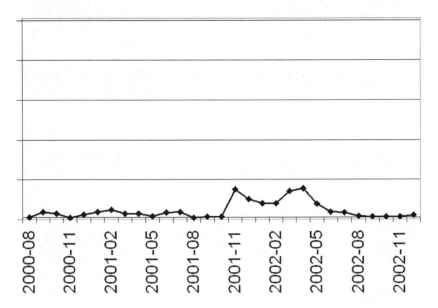

Then the unbelievably awesome tremendous news came that a baby was on the way! Wow! We were so excited! I also knew that this news was going to impact the family's finances because Jenn and I were committed to her becoming a stay-at-home mom. Now, I had been complaining that teachers were not paid enough (I still hold this view!), but when Jenn announced that she was expecting our first child, I began to hold the view that teachers were paid huge amounts of money! Why? Because that income was now going to disappear!

Our beautiful daughter showed up on a wonderful South Carolina November morning. It is a day that I will never forget! I cried like a baby. I was so proud! I was so moved by God's creation. I was so moved by His faithfulness to Jenn and me. I truly understood for the first time what "my Father's love" really means. It is unbreakable. It is unshakable. It is forever.

Chapter 1 – Introduction

Well, Jenny came home with the baby and began telling others that she was "retired". Very funny! We began to operate on just my income. We did adjust our spending some, but we continued to utilize the credit cards to make up for any gaps.

After three years in Anderson, I accepted a job transfer to a facility near Columbia, South Carolina. We sold our house in Anderson and used a good portion of the equity to help pay off some of our credit cards.

It was a tough move. Jenn and I had made a lot of great friendships in Anderson and had assisted with starting up a new church that was awesome and growing. Our hearts stayed in Anderson while we lived two hours away in Columbia.

After living in Columbia for a year, we decided to move back to our home state of Indiana to live closer to our family. This required a job change so I embarked on a job search. I found a great job in northern Indiana, accepted the position, and moved back on December 1, 2002.

Time to change spending behavior ...
It was eight degrees outside with eight inches of snow on the ground, and Jenn and I were living in a hotel room. Snow was nothing new to us, but we had been living in South Carolina for the past four-and-a-half years. It was a shock to experience this weather again!

We had known that we were going to be changing employers for about six months. We had known that we were going to be moving a long distance away. Do you think we prepared for it financially? No way!

We had no clue when I was going to be paid by my new employer, so we began loading up the credit cards again. You see, Christmas was in December that year. We believed that we had to purchase stuff for our child and each other, so out came the plastic. We paid for our groceries on the credit card. We paid for regular living expenses on the credit card. It was not good! This was the THIRD time that we were loading up the credit cards! We had taken multiple years worth of great tax refunds and paid credit card debt off, and here we were, loading them up again. Just writing about it makes my blood pressure go up and my face flush red! I was VERY unhappy about it!

Thoughts were going through my head. Thoughts like:

"How is this possible?" and "Why is this happening again?" and "This should not be happening!" and "This is embarrassing!" and "This has GOT to change!" and "How do I make this stop?" and "Who can I talk to that can help me with this?" and "I am a three-time loser with credit cards!"

Ever had those thoughts?

Well, Jenn and I came up with a plan. We chopped up the credit cards. We refused to sign up for any more debt – with the one exception of a home mortgage. We began to plan our spending every single month – some might call it budgeting – I would call it "telling your money what to do instead of having your money tell you what to do."

In 14 short months, we became debt-free except for our house. We have paid cash for every purchase since that time with the exception of our house. We have refused to do debt! We have built a savings account that we never even dreamed was possible!

7

Savings Account Balances (BEFORE & AFTER Debt Freedom!)

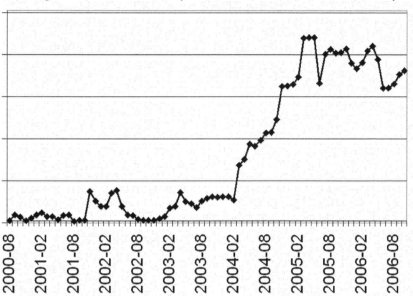

We no longer have stress related to our finances. We have financial freedom. Our marriage is better than ever! We are committed to work together on our plans for spending our money. We are able to dream because we are not stuck in the proverbial hamster wheel spinning away and getting nowhere.

I have been able to leave corporate America and pursue my life's passion of "helping others accomplish far more than they ever thought possible!" I was able to negotiate myself a massive pay cut and *smile* about it because our money is under control.

We are teaching our daughter how to manage money well. There is money in her college fund. She is saving money for her first car – and she started when she was only 4 years old!

We have money saved for a nice used car when our car finally breaks. With two ten-year-old vehicles, Jenn is starting to root for a major failure!

We have been able to give more money away than we ever dreamed we would be able to give! We are able to tithe more than the full 10% to our church. We are able to give money to Purdue University. We are able to support missionaries. We are able to support causes that we deeply believe in.

We have money available in case of an emergency! Anytime something breaks like an appliance or car, we just have an appliance or car problem. We don't have an appliance problem AND a money problem. We don't have a car problem AND a money problem.

Our retirement savings account is growing nicely. We will be able to retire some day without relying on Social Security. That is so cool!

This book will share the details of how Jenn and I got there. If I could, I would jump out from this book and encourage you by saying, "Stick with this book. Read it. Apply this stuff. You can do this!"

YOU CAN DO THIS!

I believe that every single person who reads this book can apply this stuff and take their finances to the next level. It might take a little longer for some, but I believe you can become debt-free including the house and give more than you have ever given, save more than you have ever saved, and spend more than you have ever spent!

You can accomplish far more than you ever thought possible!

When you do, I hope that you will pay it forward by helping someone else achieve financial freedom!

By the way, in case you missed it, I believe in you!

2 The Catalyst For Change

It had happened again. The bills were due, it was Christmastime, and we had no extra money. We had enough money to pay the bills OR to buy Christmas gifts, but we did not have enough to do both.

"How on earth had we arrived at this point again?!!!" I thought to myself as I was writing out the checks for that month.

It was more than a little embarrassing to discuss the matter with Jenn because this was not the first time I had to approach her about this same issue.

"Jenn," I said miserably. "We do not have enough money to pay the bills AND buy Christmas gifts."

"In fact," I continued, "I do not know when my new job will pay me, so we need to start putting ALL of our expenses on the credit card to ensure we do not run out of money."

What a horrible discussion that was. Here I was, an engineer making an excellent salary, and we had no money.

"How could this be?" I wondered.

"How could this be?" Jenn wondered.

What did we do? We used the credit card for the entire month of December. This is the same credit card that we had already paid off twice before. We had used multiple LARGE tax returns to pay down or pay off the credit cards. Yet, somehow, here we were again, out of money and running up the credit cards.

Something was not working. Something was wrong. Something had to change.

"What should we do?" I thought.

"What can I do differently?" I prayed.

Let me introduce you to ...
As I thought about what we could do differently, my mind drifted to a conversation I had with my brother, Mike, a year earlier. As I recalled the phone conversation, I smiled. This conversation happened while I was living in Columbia, South Carolina. I was picking out our Christmas tree in 70°F weather, wearing shorts and a short-sleeve shirt. While this is not a significant event for my Southern friends, this is a MAJOR event for a farm boy from Indiana. In Indiana there are approximately four months of frost-free weather, and December is NOT one of them!

While talking to Mike, he told me about this personal finance class he was taking. He rambled on and on about this class called *Financial Peace University*. It was put together by some guy named Dave Ramsey.

"Have you heard of him?" he asked me.

"No, I don't think I have," I responded distractedly as I picked out the Christmas tree.

"You should look it up," Mike said. "His name is Dave Ramsey."

"OK.", I had replied half-heartedly, ending the phone call.

Now, here I was a year later, suddenly very interested in what my brother had said. I could not remember the name of the guy teaching the class, but with a quick phone call to Mike, I was reminded that the guy's name was Dave Ramsey and the class was named *Financial Peace University*.

The day we made the decision ...
I went that next day to a book store and purchased Dave Ramsey's book, *Financial Peace, Revisited*. I read the entire book that night.

"You need to read this book immediately," I told Jenn as I handed it to her.

She did.

When she had completed the book, we discussed what we had read beginning with the key steps in Dave's Financial Plan, known as Baby Steps.

Dave Ramsey's Baby Steps
1. $1000 in a beginner emergency fund
2. Debt Snowball – pay off all debt except the house
3. 3 – 6 months of expenses in a fully-funded emergency fund
4. Retirement Saving – 15% of gross income into 401(k) or Roth IRA
5. College Savings
6. Pay off the house early
7. Build wealth and give it all away

That was all we needed to know. We were sick of living paycheck-to-paycheck. We were sick of not ever having any money in our savings account. What we had been doing was NOT working. We HAD to make a change.

Making it happen ...
On that very evening, Jenn and I pulled out the credit cards and cut them up. I called the credit card company and despite their strong persuasive arguments, I had the account shut down.

With the action of cutting up the credit cards, we were really declaring *together* that we were finished with debt. We were making a proclamation that from that day forward, we were going to manage our financial resources differently. It was a landmark moment in the lives of Joe and Jenn. Frankly, it was a landmark moment in the life of our daughter, Melea.

Four months later, we had a balanced budget that was written down on paper.

Fourteen months later, we were debt-free except for our house. In just five additional months, we had fully-funded our emergency fund.

In a total of twenty-six months, we were able to complete a replacement car fund.

In the meantime, we were able to start funding Melea's 529 college fund. Once the replacement car fund was completed, we were able to double the monthly contribution to the college fund!

Upon completion of the replacement car fund, we also began to attack the house debt. I took a blue-print schematic of the house plan and scanned it in to my computer. I then outlined the outside walls of our house. After obtaining an outline of the house, I inserted a huge quantity of small squares into the house drawing. I counted the number of squares and divided them into the purchase price of the house. I know that every single little square equals $102.92 in principal. Every time we pay off $102.92 in principal, we get to color-in a square!

14

I told you I am a maniac! I want out of debt!

Do you want to truly understand how much of your home you own? Do this for your home! You will understand just how much debt you really have!

When we started out on this house, we did not own much of it at all! I started out by coloring in our bathroom. "A man needs to at least know that he owns his throne!" I told Jenn with a smirk.

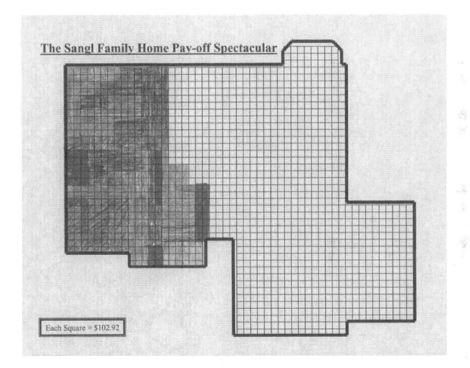

The Sangl Family Home Pay-off Spectacular

Each Square = $102.92

Commitment is tested ...
As we were working on eliminating our debt, Jenn received bad news. While on vacation in San Diego, she felt some serious stomach pains. A visit to the doctor revealed a mass. A major surgery was performed and a large tumor was removed.

It was BENIGN! PRAISE GOD!

The surgery resulted in large medical bills. We had good health insurance, but we were still responsible for a large deductible. While the bills took their four-month journey through the insurance payment process, we were able to absorb the deductible as part of our monthly budget plans and pay the bills as they arrived. Now, it DID delay our debt pay-off plans, but because we no longer had car payments, student loan payments, NO PAYMENTS EXCEPT THE HOUSE, we were able to absorb this major expense.

Ten months later, the tumors were back. Another major surgery. Another BENIGN report – PRAISE GOD! More large medical bills. We were again able to absorb the major expense.

THIS IS WHY I DO NOT ACCEPT EXCUSES!

If Jenn and I could weather the storms our finances have faced, you can too! I believe that it is all about your attitude toward your debts!

You can do this!
You may be reading this and may believe that this is not possible for you. I am here to tell you that THIS IS POSSIBLE! THIS IS REAL! This was done on a single income. This was accomplished because Jenn and I decided *together* that what we had been doing was NOT ACCEPTABLE. This was possible because Jenn and I decided *together* that we were not effectively managing the resources that God had provided us. This happened because Jenn and I decided *together* to do something about it. We committed *together* to change *our* behavior.

Beyond our decision and beyond our commitment, we actually did something different. As a result, our lives will NEVER be the same!

Jenn and I have learned a lot about our finances as we have journeyed through this together, but even better, we have learned a lot about each other. We have a much better marriage because we are working together on our finances.

Does any of this sound familiar to you? Do you feel clueless about your finances? Do you want to learn about how to achieve financial freedom? Are you tired of living paycheck-to-paycheck? Are you sick of fighting about money with your spouse? Have you been burned by debt? Are you looking for a way out?

The Critical Question
Have you reached a point where you are willing to make a major change to the way you manage your money?

If you are ready, then this book has been written for you! It is time for YOU to achieve your own financial freedom story.

Psst – I believe in you!

3 There Must Be A Plan!

You MUST have a plan for your life in order to win with your finances!

Any business person will tell you that planning is very crucial to achieving your goals!

Let's look at it this way.

Football Games
Here in South Carolina, we have these two universities that have a HUGE rivalry. These two teams are Clemson University and the University of South Carolina. Now, it is an intense rivalry no matter how you look at it, but it becomes white-hot burning craziness when you put these two schools together on a football field.

Question for you. Do you think that these two schools just show up on gameday and start thinking about what they are going to do on the field?

NOT A CHANCE!!! From the day of last year's game, a game plan for next year's match is being put together. They know which players are graduating. They know which players will still be there. They start planning accordingly.

In fact, there are multiple plans being put together! In fact, I checked out the Clemson Tigers football staff. They have a head coach, an offensive coordinator, running backs coach, offensive line coach, wide receivers coach, tight ends coach, defensive coordinator, defensive line coach, linebackers coach, and a defensive ends coach. This is just the coaches!!! You should see the list of coaching assistants!!!

From the day of the last game to the day of next year's game, they are PLANNING. All of this effort for one day, one game!

House
Would you build a house without a detailed set of plans? I am the son of a homebuilder. I can tell you that there are pages and pages of plans before the first hole is dug and the first nail is hammered! There are schematics of the finished house, foundation plans, framing plans, and HVAC and electrical plans.

It would be crazy to put that much money into a house without putting together a plan first. Wouldn't it?

Surgery
What if you needed knee surgery?

If you met with the surgeon and he said, "I'm not really sure what I am going to do. I think I am just going to start cutting on you and see whether or not we can fix this. I hope it works out."

Would you hang around? NOT A CHANCE!!! If a doctor said something like that to me, I would leave a vapor-trail getting out of the office!

I want that surgeon to KNOW FOR SURE what he is going to do. In fact, I want that surgeon to know for sure what he is going to do if there is an unexpected event that takes place while I am in surgery!!!

I want the surgeon to have a detailed plan!

Wedding
Ever been to a wedding that was not planned? Enough said!

19

War

Would you go to war without a plan? Making up a plan in the midst of bombs, gun-fire, and tanks cruising in on you really is not much fun!

So, IF football teams plan ALL YEAR for ONE GAME, and IF you would put together detailed house plans, and IF you would demand a surgeon have a plan for your surgery, and IF you would plan a wedding, and IF you would plan your strategy for war, WHY ON EARTH would you not plan your finances?

WHY? It is CRAZY to not plan your finances!!! Your financial condition will dictate your ability to accomplish your God-given hopes and dreams!

Most young people today will have more than $2,000,000 paid to them in their lifetime. SURELY the management of this money should be planned!

I believe that I have sufficiently proven the need for a plan for your finances!

There are two things necessary for you to plan your finances effectively.
1. A clear understanding of WHY you want to achieve financial freedom
2. A monthly written plan for your spending (yes – a budget – It's EZ™!)

Psst – I believe in you!

4   Why Do You Want Financial Freedom?

"What's your fuel?", a friend of mine, Mike Yoder, once asked me.

"Pardon me?" I questioned.

"Why are you doing this with your finances? What's driving you?" Mike asked. "What is your fuel?"

I have thought a lot about Mike's question. Why would someone pursue financial freedom? What are the reasons a person would want freedom from debt? Why would they wait until they had enough money to pay cash for an item instead of buying it now by using debt?

I believe that the answer is NOT "To get rich!"

"To get rich!" is not the "fuel" for most people.

I believe that for most people, the "fuel" for becoming financially free includes items like (check all that apply):

☐ Spouse can work part-time or quit job entirely to stay at home to raise the children.

☐ Adopt a child.

☐ Eliminate the STRESS of paycheck-to-paycheck living.

☐ Quit a job that "just pays the bills" and pursue a job that they were put on this earth to do and are passionate about!

☐ Obtain the ability to do what one is made to do *regardless* of the income potential!

☐ Start up the business they have always dreamed of.

- ☐ Pay bills one time per month.
- ☐ Spouse can go back to college.
- ☐ Go do exactly what they have been put on Earth to do regardless of the income.
- ☐ Children will be able to go to college.
- ☐ Daughter can have a beautiful wedding.
- ☐ Support meaningful causes that you value and <u>want</u> to support financially.
- ☐ Quit the job that requires one to work a lot of overtime and take a job that earns less, but allows more time with family.
- ☐ Retire!
- ☐ Give themselves a raise by managing their money better.
- ☐ Vacations that are paid for in advance!
- ☐ Own a few of life's pleasures.
- ☐ Eliminate money fights.
- ☐ Improved marriage.
- ☐ Start a non-profit organization to help others (orphanage, university, crisis pregnancy center, etc.)

These are all AWESOME reasons to pursue financial freedom! These reasons are all value-focused. They are focused on the values that YOU hold highly.

Ask yourself this question …

If you stay in debt, will you be prevented from accomplishing your dreams?

Do you have big dreams? Dreams you would not even reveal to anyone for fear of the response? If you stay in debt, the chance is great that you will never be able to pursue that dream because your time will not be yours to govern. You will have to go to WORK to pay the bills.

I am personally done with WORK. I am no longer doing WORK. In fact, I refuse to do WORK. I am now CRUSADING! I am championing a CAUSE! I am SICK of seeing people live paycheck-to-paycheck. I am SICK of seeing people WITHOUT HOPE. I am SICK of meeting people who have given up on their dreams all because they exchanged them for the big lie that the $40,000 car and the $10,000 TV/Sound System would make them happy. I am here to help the HOPELESS become HOPEFUL. I am here to help the DEBT-RIDDEN become DEBT-FREE! I will NOT accept the "I will always have a car payment" mentality! I will NOT listen quietly to another person tell me that "I could never become financially free!"

BOGUS!!! UNACCEPTABLE!!! BOO TO YOU! DOWN WITH YOU! DOWN WITH THE "POOR ME" ATTITUDE!

IT DOES NOT HAVE TO BE THAT WAY!!!

Do you want to achieve your dreams? Do you want to achieve financial freedom? Read on! Apply this stuff! Put together a plan that takes you from where you are to where you want to be! Write it down! Put it on the refrigerator! Make it highly visible! Get real! If you want to achieve the thing you were put on this earth to do, you have got to have a plan. It will not just happen! Make it happen! If God called you to do it, by all means **GO DO IT!!!**

Before you move on to the next chapter, take five minutes to list YOUR reasons for wanting to achieve financial freedom. When you are done, I recommend that you tear it out and place it on your refrigerator!

Psst – I believe in you!

Dreaming …
In our lifetime, we want to …

5 It's EZ™ To Budget!

Budget???!!! PLEASE do not close the book now. PLEASE do not burn this book. PLEASE read on! I promise you that this material will change your life!

When I ask people if they have a budget, they get this problem with the corners of their lips. Their lips tend to form a sneer as they respond with a resounding "NO!"

I have found that for many people, the word "budget" is a very close relative to many 4-letter words. It became this way because of past experiences.

They have tried budgeting in the past, and it did not work for them.

They were handed a budget by their spouse and were told that they were required to live by it. The budget had $3.45 budgeted for dining out and $5.31 for groceries and had nothing for school clothes for the kids. As a result, the budget was not feasible.

Trust me on this. You will never regret the decision to have a monthly budget.

Here is why I say this ...

My journey to financial freedom would not have been possible without a monthly budget!

In every family, it seems that there is a spender and a saver. In our family, I was the spender and Jenn was the saver. I, however, managed the finances because this allowed me to have control and to be able to spend anything we had that was extra. BAD PLAN!

Anyway, we had now made the commitment to work *together* on our finances. It was four months after making this commitment to each other that Jenn came walking in to the living room with a piece of paper. "What do you think of this budget?" she asked, interrupting the TV program I was watching.

A sneer automatically formed on my face as I said, "A budget?"

I was thinking, "A budget? I don't need no stinking budget!"

"We need something to make our money behave," Jenny said.

Now, there are times in life that you will have magic moments. Moments that you will look back on and note as landmarks in your life. Moments that will change your entire future. Jenn had just created a landmark moment in the life of the Sangl family. She had latched us onto THE item that would allow us to win with our finances. I am forever grateful to Jenn for doing this. She did not write up the budget to get what she wanted. She did not write it up to control me. It was developed so *we* could win with our finances *together*.

MARRIED GUYS who are reading this book take this note: Your wife is VERY WISE and when she approaches you with an idea it should be treated as very valuable.

A prior attempt at budgeting ...
I had tried budgeting before. It was an annual budget. I put the budget together to try to convince Jenn that we could purchase a brand new Honda Odyssey.

Income Item	Yearly	Monthly $	Category	
Joe	$ 70,700.00	$ 5,891.67	Income	
Jen	$ -	$ -	Income	
Total Income	$ 70,700.00	$ 5,891.67		
Expense Item	Yearly	Monthly $	Category	
Automobile - 1997 Truck	$ 3,000.00	$ 250.00	Auto	✓
Automobile - Mini-van	$ 6,600.00	$ 550.00	Auto	
Gasoline	$ 1,400.00	$ 116.67	Auto	✓
Insurance	$ 1,000.00	$ 83.33	Auto	_Could lower._
Maintenance	$ 1,000.00	$ 83.33	Auto	✓
Cable Television	$ 600.00	$ 50.00	Utility	_Could not get._
Electricity	$ 700.00	$ 58.33	Utility	✓
Garbage & Recycle	$ 180.00	$ 15.00	Utility	✓
Internet	$ 264.00	$ 22.00	Utility	_Could not get._
Natural Gas	$ 860.00	$ 71.67	Utility	✓
Telephone	$ 1,000.00	$ 83.33	Utility	✓
Water & Sewer	$ 500.00	$ 41.67	Utility	✓
Tithes	$ 7,100.00	$ 591.67	Charity	✓
Purdue University	$ 100.00	$ 8.33	Charity	✓
United Way	$ 780.00	$ 65.00	Charity	✓
Groceries	$ 5,200.00	$ 433.33	Food	_Could we lower?_
Dining Out	$ 1,000.00	$ 83.33	Food	✓
Gifts	$ 1,000.00	$ 83.33	Gifts	✓
Healthcare	$ 500.00	$ 41.67	Health	✓
Household	$ 1,000.00	$ 83.33	Household	✓
Health Insurance	$ 1,500.00	$ 125.00	Insurance	✓
Life Insurance	$ 530.00	$ 44.17	Insurance	✓
Mortgage	$ 10,800.00	$ 900.00	House	✓
YMCA	$ 700.00	$ 58.33	Health	_Could we lower?_
Miscellaneous Spending	$ 4,000.00	$ 333.33	Misc	_Could we lower._
Vacation	$ 3,000.00	$ 250.00	Vacation	
Taxes	$ 20,000.00	$ 1,666.67	Taxes	
Clothing	$ 1,000.00	$ 83.33	Clothes	
401k	$ 5,656.00	$ 471.33	Investment	
Total Required	$ 80,970.00	$ 6,747.50		
Delta	$ (10,270.00)	$ (855.83)		

My Horrible Attempt At Annual Budgeting

Take a look at the budget. It does not even come close to balancing! Instead of addressing the HUGE car payment I was trying to put into the budget, I was cutting out expenses that really did not amount to much. It was the classic case of ignoring the elephant in the room! We ended up not getting the car. Again it was due to my listening to Jenn and her wise advice. My budget had failed (to get me the car), so I had a bad feeling about budgets.

So here Jenn was trying to convince me to try budgeting again. Although I did not feel like budgeting, I felt that I should give it a try because my cute wife had written it down! The least I could do was look at the budget. And here is that budget.

Sangl Family's First-Ever Budget

One look at the budget got my attention. There was something highly unusual about this budget. It did not require debt to live that month! It did not require the credit card which was good since we had chopped those up months ago!

Now I am a spender, but I am also a nerd. I saw an immediate possibility that we could use Microsoft Excel to prepare the budget. Microsoft Excel spreadsheets have the capability to automatically update the math as you adjust the income and expenses. It allows you to focus on "what" you are spending instead of conducting multiple math exercises on a calculator.

As I prepared the budget in Microsoft Excel, I realized the MOST POWERFUL LESSON I have ever learned about managing my personal finances.

I have a diploma from Southwestern High School, a Bachelor of Science in Mechanical Engineering from Purdue University, and a Masters of Business Administration from Clemson University, but I had never learned this lesson before. I had taken **20 years** of formal education and never learned this lesson. **TWENTY YEARS!!!**

Are you ready for the lesson I learned? Do NOT underestimate the POWER of this lesson. It may seem really simple to you. It may seem really juvenile. It might even be so ridiculously easy that you might think I am joking.

I am NOT joking.

If you get this lesson and apply it to your finances, you will win. If you do not apply it to your finances, your chances of succeeding will drop dramatically. No one is exempt from this lesson. It is a hard and fast rule!

Are you ready for the lesson that changed my life?

The lesson that forever changed Joe and Jenn Sangl's lives:

INCOME – OUTGO = EXACTLY ZERO^{TM}

$$I - O = EZ^{TM}$$

$$It's\ EZ^{TM}!$$

INCOME – OUTGO = EXACTLY ZERO^{TM}

No matter who you are, you cannot avoid this fact. The last I checked, money did not grow on trees. It is finite. It is limited. There really is only a known amount of it.

You might make $1,000 a month. You might make $5,000 a month. You might even make $20,000 a month. I don't care what the amount is. The fact is that it is a limited amount.

If you make $20,000 a month and spend $20,000 of it, I can guarantee you that you will have $0 left! If you make $20,000 and spend $21,000, I can guarantee that you will have had to reduce your savings by $1,000 or utilize debt to spend the $1,000.

Now, you could use a printer to print $1,000 in money, but you will be introduced to a new home that comes complete with room and board – it is called jail! The $1,000 will NOT jump out of thin air to make up the difference. Only the federal government can legally print money.

What is the amount you make each month? Whatever it is, it is limited! That is a fact! Stop whining about needing to earn more before you can start saving. The facts are the facts! If you spend more than you made this month, you did one of two things to make up the difference: (1) burned through your savings or (2) used debt. Money just does not grow on trees!

INCOME – OUTGO = EXACTLY ZERO^{TM}

Look at that formula. I am an engineer. I am used to derivatives, integrations, kernels, and other complex items. This formula just seems too simple!

I am here to tell you that it is really is just that simple!

Budgeting software that is demonstrated on the next few pages is available for FREE at www.JOESANGL.com – click on "TOOLS". The tools use Microsoft Excel. This budgeting spreadsheet will be used to teach you how to budget *your* money.

Plan your spending on paper BEFORE you receive the actual money.

Step 1: Make a list of all of your expected income and expenses for this month.

Let's say a couple named Ron and Judy wanted to start budgeting monthly. The first step is to list out their expected income and expenses.

INCOME	AMOUNT
Take Home Income	$3,000.00
OUTGO	
Charitable Gifts	$350.00
Emergency Fund	$200.00
Mortgage	$550.00
Electricity/Gas	$200.17
Water	$25.45
Cell Phone	$45.10
Trash	$15.10
Cable	$31.70
Groceries	$350.00
Dining Out	$150.00
Car Payment	$378.00
Gasoline	$150.00
License Plates	$16.67
Auto Insurance	$75.00
Oil Change	$30.00
Clothes – Children	$100.00
Doctor Bill	$125.14
Life Insurance	$40.00
Babysitting	$50.00
Spending Money	$100.00
Credit Card Bill	$125.00
Student Loan	$135.00
Entertainment (Basketball Game)	$74.00
TOTAL OUTGO	**$3316.33**

As you can see, the expenses are greater than the income this month! Does this sound familiar? The goal in this first step is to list all of your wants/needs for the month. You will make decisions on what will be included or excluded shortly!

I recommend that you write out your wants/needs for the month on paper. It is much easier for both of you to contribute to the conversation if you can both be writing on the same sheet of paper. I have included a sheet here for you to use if you so desire. You can print out a larger copy by visiting www.JOESANGL.com – click on "Tools"

EZ Budget[TM]

TOTAL INCOME	
TOTAL OUTGO	
INCOME - OUTGO	

INCOME (Take Home Pay)	Amount
Income 1	
Income 2	
Income 3	
Income 4	

OUTGO (Actual Expenses)	Amount
Giving	
Charitable Organizations	
Gifts	
Christmas Gifts	

Saving	Amount
Emergency Fund	
Retirement Fund	
New Car Fund	
New Furniture Fund	
College Fund	
Wedding Fund	
Other:	
Other:	

Housing	Amount
Mortgage – 1st	
Mortgage – 2nd	
Rent	
Homeowner's Insurance	
Renter's Insurance	
Property Taxes	
Homeowner's Association Fees	
Electricity	
Natural Gas	
Telephone	
Cable TV – Satellite TV	
Internet	
Water	
Sewer	
Trash	
Other:	
Other:	

Transportation	Amount
Car Payment – 1	
Car Payment – 2	
Car Insurance	
Car License Plate Fees/Taxes	
Gasoline/Diesel	
Car Repairs	
Oil Change/Maintenance	
Other:	
Other:	

Chapter 5 – It's EZ^{TM} To Budget!

Food	Amount
Groceries	
Dining Out	
School Lunches	
Other:	

Clothing	Amount
Children	
Adults	
Other:	

Other Debts	Amount
Credit Card 1	
Credit Card 2	
Credit Card 3	
Credit Card 4	
Credit Card 5	
Student Loan 1	
Student Loan 2	
Student Loan 3	
Furniture	
Other:	
Other:	
Other:	
Other:	
Other:	
Other:	

Personal	Amount
Health Insurance	
Life Insurance	
Child Care	
Alimony	
Child Support	
Vacation	
Income Taxes	
Entertainment	
Cell Phone	
Medical Bill	
Spending Money	
Other:	
Other:	
Other:	

Step 2: Enter the expenses into the budgeting program.
After you have written the expenses out onto the sheet, it is time
to enter them in to the budgeting program. NOTE: You could
prepare your budget on paper, but TRUST ME when I say it is
SO MUCH *EASIER* to enter the numbers into a program, and
have it do the math for you!

TOTAL INCOME	3,000.00
TOTAL OUTGO	3,316.33
INCOME - OUTGO	-316.33

INCOME (Take Home Pay)	Amount
Income 1	3,000

OUTGO (Actual Expenses)	Amount
Giving	
Charitable Organizations	350.00

Saving	Amount
Emergency Fund	200.00

Housing	Amount
Mortgage – 1st	550.00
Electricity	200.17
Cable TV – Satellite TV	31.70
Water	25.45
Trash	15.10

Transportation	Amount
Car Payment – 1	378.00
Car Insurance	75.00
Car License Plate Fees/Taxes	16.67
Gasoline/Diesel	150.00
Oil Change/Maintenance	30.00

Food	Amount
Groceries	350.00
Dining Out	150.00

Clothing	Amount
Children	100.00

Other Debts	Amount
Credit Card 1	125.00
Student Loan 1	135.00

Personal	Amount
Life Insurance	40.00
Child Care	50.00
Entertainment	74.00
Cell Phone	45.10
Medical Bill	125.14
Spending Money	100.00

As you can see very clearly now, the OUTGO exceeds the INCOME by $316.33. This is not an EZ Budget™. Are you starting to see the power of putting every expense on paper BEFORE the income arrives? If you tried to budget AFTER you have received the income, your money would not necessarily be going where you really want it to go.

By putting every dollar on paper PRIOR to receiving the income and PRIOR to incurring the expenses, you will be given the POWER to make a choice on where your money goes. You will have CONTROL of your finances! That is awesome! I told you that you could do this! This is not hard! Go ahead! YELL OUT LOUD, "I CAN DO THIS!!!"

I had a class in junior high school called "I Can!". The course was written by the renowned motivational speaker Zig Ziglar. I have never forgotten those two words – "I CAN!" Guess what? "YOU CAN!" I believe in you! I have seen MANY people who thought "I can't" have their lives dramatically transformed through the application of this budget process. They now understand that Henry Ford was right when he said, "Whether you think you can or you can't, you're right!"

Step 3: Make INCOME – OUTGO = EXACTLY ZERO™
Remember the formula? Here it is again! I really want you to get this! If you get nothing else out of this book, I want you to get this formula! It's EZ™!

INCOME – OUTGO = EXACTLY ZERO™

We have entered the income and expected expenses, and you see that Ron and Judy are upside down $316.33. Now, Ron and Judy *could* live by this budget this month, couldn't they? But they would have to do one of the two things discussed earlier: (1) burn savings or (2) use debt.

Ron and Judy have committed to each other that they are going to win with their money. They are ready to make a change that really works for them and will help them achieve their long-term goals. This means that they are going to have to increase the income or reduce the outgo this month.

There is little opportunity for Ron to increase his income this month since he receives a monthly salary. Judy is focused on raising their children. As a result, income is set for this month. Ron is going to bring home $3,000. This is Ron's take-home pay. This is after paying taxes, health insurance, retirement contributions, etc. The $3,000 is what will be available to spend.

Since the income is not going to increase this month, the adjustments must be made to the outgo. This means that $316.33 must be removed from the expected expenses for the month.

INCOME – OUTGO = EXACTLY ZERO^{TM}

Let's review their expenses to understand what is absolutely necessary. Take a moment to review their expected expenses. What do you think is absolutely necessary?

Now, this may vary a little from person-to-person, but at a minimum I believe that the following items are necessary expenses.
- o Housing (plus utilities for the house – does NOT include luxuries like cable TV!)
- o Transportation (gas, car payment, car insurance – does not include four car washes a month!)
- o Food (ensure that you and the children have enough to eat and be healthy – does not include restaurants!)
- o Clothing (ensure that you and the children have appropriate clothing – does not include the latest and greatest fashions or brands of clothing!)

Chapter 5 – It's EZ^{TM} To Budget!

In Ron and Judy's case, they are able to pay these expenses. Their problem is like the vast majority of Americans. Their "wants list' exceeds their ability to pay for them. Now, unlike the average American, Ron and Judy are committed to making this an EZ Budget^{TM}.

What expenses should they cut?

I could ask 100 people that question, and I would get 100 different answers. We are all different from each other. We value different things. The way in which we make decisions is different. This is OK as long as we end up with an EZ Budget^{TM}.

So what did Ron and Judy do?

Well, Ron and Judy thought that they could cut back on their "Spending Money". They reduced it from $100 to $50. That made the budget deficit equal to $266.33.

TOTAL INCOME	3,000.00
TOTAL OUTGO	3,266.33
INCOME – OUTGO	-266.33

Ron and Judy then decided that instead of attending a basketball game and a movie this month, they would attend the basketball game but just watch some movies at home instead. They reduced their "Entertainment" fund from $74 to $35. Their budget is now only $227.33 short.

TOTAL INCOME	3,000.00
TOTAL OUTGO	3,227.33
INCOME – OUTGO	-227.33

Ron and Judy had $50 budgeted for childcare. They decided to exchange babysitting with Ken and Meg. No cost. Bartering!!! I love it!! That reduced the deficit another $50. This is close to being EZ^{TM}!

TOTAL INCOME	3,000.00
TOTAL OUTGO	3,177.33
INCOME – OUTGO	-177.33

The children really did have enough clothes, but it would be nice to buy a pair of shoes for one of them. Ron and Judy reduced the "Clothing" fund to $50. The gap is now $127.33!

TOTAL INCOME	3,000.00
TOTAL OUTGO	3,127.33
INCOME – OUTGO	-127.33

Dining out is fun, but Ron and Judy really are committed to getting out of debt and winning with their finances. They decided to eat out one less time and reduced their "Dining Out" fund to $100. The budget now stands at $77.33 short. CLOSE!

TOTAL INCOME	3,000.00
TOTAL OUTGO	3,077.33
INCOME – OUTGO	-77.33

The grocery fund has previously absorbed a few movies that jumped into the cart at Wal-Mart. This month, Ron and Judy have decided together that they will not let that happen. They reduced the grocery budget by $50 to $300. WOW! Only $27.33 away!

TOTAL INCOME	3,000.00
TOTAL OUTGO	3,027.33
INCOME – OUTGO	-27.33

The oil change was for the car, and it has only been 3,000 miles. Ron and Judy decided to wait one month. The car could go one extra month without any real issue. The budget is now $2.67 FAVORABLE!!!

TOTAL INCOME	3,000.00
TOTAL OUTGO	2,997.33
INCOME – OUTGO	+2.67

To give EVERY DOLLAR a name, Ron and Judy added the $2.67 back to the "Entertainment" fund taking it from $35.00 to $37.67.

TOTAL INCOME	3,000.00
TOTAL OUTGO	3,000.00
INCOME – OUTGO	0.00

OH MY GOODNESS!!! What just happened??!! Ron and Judy just made INCOME – OUTGO = EXACTLY ZERO!!!!!!!! It is now an EZ Budget™!!!

INCOME – OUTGO = EXACTLY ZERO^TM

TOTAL INCOME	3,000.00
TOTAL OUTGO	3,000.00
INCOME - OUTGO	0.00

INCOME (Take Home Pay)	Amount
Income 1	3,000

OUTGO (Actual Expenses)	Amount
Giving	
Charitable Organizations	350.00

Saving	Amount
Emergency Fund	200.00

Housing	Amount
Mortgage – 1st	550.00
Electricity	200.17
Cable TV – Satellite TV	31.70
Water	25.45
Trash	15.10

Transportation	Amount
Car Payment – 1	378.00
Car Insurance	75.00
Car License Plate Fees/Taxes	16.67
Gasoline/Diesel	150.00
Oil Change/Maintenance	0.00

Food	Amount
Groceries	300.00
Dining Out	100.00

Clothing	Amount
Children	50.00

Other Debts	Amount
Credit Card 1	125.00
Student Loan 1	135.00

Personal	Amount
Life Insurance	40.00
Child Care	0.00
Entertainment	37.67
Cell Phone	45.10
Medical Bill	125.14
Spending Money	50.00

Did you see how that worked? Did you see how Ron and Judy had to make some choices? I must say again that Ron and Judy did not *have* to make their budget balance. They could have thrown in $316.33 from savings and made the budget "balance". They could have used their credit cards to pay for $316.33 of their expenses and made the budget "balance", but they have had enough. They have realized that the equation really is TRUE!

INCOME – OUTGO = EXACTLY ZERO^{TM}

Ron and Judy have learned the single most powerful lesson I have learned about finances. You will not win until you make your money behave. The ONLY way I have found that makes this happen is through a written budget.

They will still be able to live and live well on this budget!

How long do you think this process will take you the first time you put together a budget like this? It will probably take you less time than you think. I have found that it takes between 45 and 60 minutes to make your first EZ Budget^{TM}.

After someone has done this for three months in a row, it will take an average of 20 minutes to put together the entire spending plan for the month! ONLY TWENTY MINUTES!!!

TWENTY MINUTES THAT WILL CHANGE YOUR ENTIRE FINANCIAL FUTURE!!! TWENTY MINUTES THAT WILL ALLOW YOU TO RETIRE SOMEDAY!!! TWENTY MINUTES THAT WILL ALLOW YOUR WIFE TO STAY AT HOME AND RAISE THE CHILDREN!!! TWENTY MINUTES THAT WILL ENABLE YOU TO PAY FOR YOUR CHILDREN'S COLLEGE! TWENTY MINUTES TO ACCOMPLISH YOUR DREAMS!

You spent more than twenty minutes thinking about where you are going to go eat lunch today!

Step 4: Live according to the EZ Budget^{TM}.
If Ron and Judy prepared this budget and then went out and began to spend money on other items, this budget would not work. Why? They added expenses without taking away others. Money does not grow on trees. Therefore, they will burn savings

or turn to debt to make up the difference. They have also just wasted time preparing the budget.

If you are *not* going to live by the budget you prepare, I just have one question:

WHY BOTHER?

I am serious! Why bother? If you just went through the trouble to read this book, put together an EZ Budget™, and are now going to ignore what you have prepared, why bother? Burn this book! Go ahead and live with debt for another five years. See if it is your friend. I have been there. I have prepared a budget that did not balance, and I did not live by it. Guess what? IT DID NOT WORK!!! Big surprise!

Believe me, debt is not your friend!

You may not know anyone else who puts together a budget. Guess what? They are probably BROKE! They are certainly not doing as well as they could with their finances. The act of writing out your spending BEFORE you ever spend the money is SO POWERFUL! It enables you to take CONTROL of your finances. It enables you to make CHOICES about your spending!

I will borrow Nike's marketing slogan as it pertains to your monthly EZ Budget™... **JUST DO IT!**

How to Budget – Final Notes
Let's review the steps again.
Step 1: Make a list of all of your expected income and expenses for this month.
Step 2: Enter the expenses into the budgeting program.
Step 3: Make INCOME – OUTGO = EXACTLY ZERO™.
Step 4: Live according to the EZ Budget™.

You can do this! Trust me! I was able to do it! When I realized that this was the ticket for Jenn and me to become debt-free, I was willing to walk over hot coals to do it. It ended up being the ticket for our marriage to become unbelievably better!

If you haven't already, go ahead and create your own EZ Budget^{TM}! You are on your way to financial freedom!!!

Free copies of budgets are available at www.JOESANGL.com Click on "TOOLS".

Psst – I believe in you!

6 Weekly Budgeting

Regardless of how often you are paid or how much you are paid, the fact remains that:

INCOME – OUTGO = EXACTLY ZERO™

Monthly budgeting is admittedly the easiest form of budgeting. However, I fully understand that most persons just getting started on this journey to financial freedom are unable to sit down and write out all of the checks once a month and be done with it (I was there!).

For most persons, there is this balancing act that is played out every single month. Each paycheck pays certain bills. For many couples that are paid twice a month, one of the pay periods is a period of "famine" and the other pay period is a period of "feast". This does not have to be!

This chapter will show you how to budget when you are paid weekly, bi-monthly, every two weeks, or have any other pay schedule that delivers income to your household throughout the month.

Let's go back to Ron and Judy's balanced budget. Let's assume that they are paid $750/week take-home pay. They do not have enough money in their account to just sit down and write out all of the checks at once. This means that they must balance their spending to align with the arrival of each paycheck.

Below are Ron and Judy's expenses for the month.

INCOME	AMOUNT	When?	
Take Home Income	3,000.00	$750/week	
OUTGO			
Charitable Gifts	350.00	All Month	
Emergency Fund	200.00	All Month	
Mortgage	550.00	15th	
Electricity/Gas	200.17	10th	
Water	25.45	15th	
Cell Phone	45.10	25th	
Trash	15.10	15th	
Cable	31.70	15th	
Groceries	300.00	All Month	
Dining Out	100.00	All Month	
Car Payment	378.00	10th	
Gasoline	150.00	All Month	
License Plates	16.67	Saving	$200/yr ($16.67/mo)
Auto Insurance	75.00	15th	
Oil Change		When Possible	
Clothes – Children	50.00	When Possible	
Doctor Bill	125.14	10th	
Life Insurance	40.00	10th	$480/yr ($40/mo)
Babysitting		When Possible	
Spending Money	50.00	All Month	
Credit Card Bill	125.00	20th	
Student Loan	135.00	10th	
Entertainment (Basketball Game)	37.67	When Possible	
TOTAL OUTGO	**3000.00**		

Using the Monthly Budget By Week found FREE at www.JOESANGL.com (click on "TOOLS"), Ron and Judy loaded their planned expenses into the approximate date that each bill was due.

Monthly EZ Budget™ – Weekly

	10/29	11/5	11/12	11/19	TOTAL
TOTAL INCOME	750.00	750.00	750.00	750.00	3,000.00
TOTAL OUTGO	625.31	983.02	912.50	479.17	3,000.00
INCOME - OUTGO	+124.69	-233.02	-162.50	+270.83	0.00
INCOME (Take Home Pay)	Amount	Amount	Amount	Amount	Amount
Income 1	750.00	750.00	750.00	750.00	3,000.00
OUTGO (Actual Expenses)					
Giving	Amount	Amount	Amount	Amount	Amount
Charitable Organizations	87.50	87.50	87.50	87.50	350.00
Saving	Amount	Amount	Amount	Amount	Amount
Emergency Fund	50.00	50.00	50.00	50.00	200.00
Housing	Amount	Amount	Amount	Amount	Amount
Mortgage – 1st			550.00		550.00
Electricity		200.17			200.17
Cable TV – Satellite TV		31.70			31.70
Water		25.45			25.45
Trash		15.10			15.10
Transportation	Amount	Amount	Amount	Amount	Amount
Car Payment – 1		378.00			378.00
Car Insurance			75.00		75.00
Car License Plate Fees/Taxes				16.67	16.67
Gasoline/Diesel	37.50	37.50	37.50	37.50	150.00
Oil Change/Maintenance					0.00
Food	Amount	Amount	Amount	Amount	Amount
Groceries	75.00	75.00	75.00	75.00	300.00
Dining Out	25.00	25.00	25.00	25.00	100.00
Clothing	Amount	Amount	Amount	Amount	Amount
Children				50.00	50.00
Other Debts	Amount	Amount	Amount	Amount	Amount
Credit Card 1				125.00	125.00
Student Loan 1	135.00				135.00
Personal	Amount	Amount	Amount	Amount	Amount
Life Insurance	40.00				40.00
Child Care	0.00				0.00
Entertainment	37.67				37.67
Cell Phone		45.10			45.10
Medical Bill	125.14				125.14
Spending Money	12.50	12.50	12.50	12.50	50.00

Ron and Judy's budget is an EZ Budget™ overall. However, each week does not equal exactly zero. Knowing that money does not grow on trees, this is a problem!

Ron and Judy are confident that the overall budget will work, but now they must develop an individual EZ Budget™ for each paycheck.

Ron and Judy's 11/5 and 11/12 paychecks were overspent while the 10/29 and 11/19 paychecks were underspent. They began to look for areas where expenses could be moved from 11/5 and 11/12 to the 10/29 and 11/19 paychecks.

Ron and Judy decided to move their Emergency Buffer Fund savings from the 10/29, 11/5, and 11/12 paychecks to the 11/29 paycheck.

	10/29	11/5	11/12	11/29	TOTAL
TOTAL INCOME	750.00	750.00	750.00	750.00	3,000.00
TOTAL OUTGO	575.31	933.02	862.50	629.17	3,000.00
INCOME – OUTGO	+174.69	-183.02	-112.50	+120.83	0.00

	10/29	11/5	11/12	11/29	TOTAL
Emergency Buffer Fund	0.00	0.00	0.00	200.00	200.00

Ron and Judy moved $174.69 of their $378 Car Payment to 10/29. The 10/29 budget is now EZ™!

	10/29	11/5	11/12	11/29	TOTAL
TOTAL INCOME	750.00	750.00	750.00	750.00	3,000.00
TOTAL OUTGO	750.00	858.33	912.50	479.17	3,000.00
INCOME – OUTGO	0.00	-8.33	-112.50	+120.83	0.00

	10/29	11/5	11/12	11/29	TOTAL
Car Payment – 1	174.69	203.31			378.00

Ron and Judy then moved $8.33 of their Spending Money from the 11/5 paycheck to the 11/29 paycheck. The 11/5 budget is now EZ™!

	10/29	11/5	11/12	11/29	TOTAL
TOTAL INCOME	750.00	750.00	750.00	750.00	3,000.00
TOTAL OUTGO	750.00	750.00	900.00	561.77	3,000.00
INCOME – OUTGO	0.00	0.00	-112.50	+112.50	0.00

	10/29	11/5	11/12	11/29	TOTAL
Spending Money	12.50	4.17	12.50	20.83	50.00

Ron and Judy decided that they could skip one week of groceries and dining out. They had enough food in the refrigerator, freezer and cabinets that they could go an entire week without purchasing groceries. Besides, it was time to clean out the cabinets anyway. They moved the $75 grocery and $25 dining out money from the 11/12 week and added it to the 11/19 week.

	10/29	11/5	11/12	11/29	TOTAL
TOTAL INCOME	750.00	750.00	750.00	750.00	3,000.00
TOTAL OUTGO	750.00	750.00	762.50	737.50	3,000.00
INCOME – OUTGO	0.00	0.00	-12.50	+12.50	0.00
Groceries	75.00	75.00	0.00	150.00	300.00
Dining Out	25.00	25.00	0.00	50.00	100.00

Seeing the $12.50 shortage in the 11/12 budget, Ron and Judy moved $12.50 of Spending Money from the 11/12 paycheck to the 11/29 paycheck.

	10/29	11/5	11/12	11/29	TOTAL
TOTAL INCOME	750.00	750.00	750.00	750.00	3,000.00
TOTAL OUTGO	750.00	750.00	750.00	750.00	3,000.00
INCOME – OUTGO	0.00	0.00	0.00	0.00	0.00
Spending Money	12.50	4.17	0.00	33.33	300.00

SUCCESS!!! An EZ Budget™ for every single paycheck!!!

INCOME – OUTGO = EXACTLY ZERO™ for every single paycheck!

All of their payments were made on time and every single obligation was met!

Monthly EZ Budget™ – Weekly

	10/29	11/5	11/12	11/19	TOTAL
TOTAL INCOME	750.00	750.00	750.00	750.00	3,000.00
TOTAL OUTGO	750.00	750.00	750.00	750.00	3,000.00
INCOME - OUTGO	0.00	0.00	0.00	0.00	0.00
INCOME (Take Home Pay)	Amount	Amount	Amount	Amount	Amount
Income 1	750.00	750.00	750.00	750.00	3,000.00
OUTGO (Actual Expenses)					
Giving	Amount	Amount	Amount	Amount	Amount
Charitable Organizations	87.50	87.50	87.50	87.50	350.00
Saving	Amount	Amount	Amount	Amount	Amount
Emergency Fund				200.00	200.00
Housing	Amount	Amount	Amount	Amount	Amount
Mortgage – 1st			550.00		550.00
Electricity		200.17			200.17
Cable TV – Satellite TV		31.70			31.70
Water		25.45			25.45
Trash		15.10			15.10
Transportation	Amount	Amount	Amount	Amount	Amount
Car Payment – 1	174.69	203.31			378.00
Car Insurance		75.00			75.00
Car License Plate Fees/Taxes				16.67	16.67
Gasoline/Diesel	37.50	37.50	37.50	37.50	150.00
Oil Change/Maintenance					0.00
Food	Amount	Amount	Amount	Amount	Amount
Groceries	75.00	75.00		150.00	300.00
Dining Out	25.00	25.00		50.00	100.00
Clothing	Amount	Amount	Amount	Amount	Amount
Children				50.00	50.00
Other Debts	Amount	Amount	Amount	Amount	Amount
Credit Card 1				125.00	125.00
Student Loan 1	135.00				135.00
Personal	Amount	Amount	Amount	Amount	Amount
Life Insurance	40.00				40.00
Child Care	0.00				0.00
Entertainment	37.67				37.67
Cell Phone		45.10			45.10
Medical Bill	125.14				125.14
Spending Money	12.50	4.17		33.33	50.00

Now you may be saying, "Joe, how could they just skip a week without buying groceries? That is not possible!"

My answer is that Ron and Judy are no longer normal. They can easily go one week without purchasing groceries. Besides, they have a full three weeks to prepare for that one week. That means that BECAUSE THEY PLANNED, they have the opportunity to adjust their "Grocery" spending NOW. By being frugal, they will be able to have money left over in the "Grocery" fund from the 10/29 and 11/5 weeks.

Did you get the part about Ron and Judy *having a plan* BEFORE spending their money?!!! They have a PLAN before they ever receive the actual cash. I cannot emphasize this point enough! By having a plan, Ron and Judy can work together to ensure that they prepare appropriately for upcoming budget crunches.

This is the beauty of the budgeting process! You are now managing your money instead of your money managing you! You are now telling your money where to go instead of wondering where it went!

What if Ron and Judy were paid only two times during the month? They would enter their take-home income for the weeks they are paid and make the equation INCOME – OUTGO = EXACTLY ZERO™ true for each paycheck.

How to Budget Weekly or Bi-Weekly – Final Notes
Let's review the steps again.
Step 1: Make a list of all of your expected income and expenses for this month.
Step 2: Enter the expenses into the budgeting program.
Step 3: Make INCOME – OUTGO = EXACTLY ZERO™.
Step 4: Make each individual paycheck an EZ Budget™.
Step 5: Live according to the EZ Budget™.

It is that simple!!! I *love* this stuff!

It's so EZ™!

Psst – I believe in you!

7 Seasonal Budgeting

Budgeting when income is irregular/cyclical/seasonal
Many self-employed persons and business owners know all too well the facts of irregular income. If you are in the lawn-care business, the grass just stops growing in the winter and then in the summer the grass will not stop growing! If you are in the retail industry, you may experience the Christmas shopping rush and the post-Christmas drought. If you are in the tourism industry, you may experience the summer vacation crowds and the off-season slump.

It is a reality. Many people that I work with who have this type of income believe that it is impossible to budget when income is so irregular. I respond by saying that it is VERY possible and IMPERATIVE that they do budget!

Folks who have irregular income need a budget more than anyone!!!

Step 1: Recognize it!
You must recognize that you have irregular income! If you have ever starved to death during the "off" season, you KNOW what I am talking about! In order to stop having your life severely impacted by "off" seasons, you must prepare!

Step 2: Determine your monthly expenses.
To determine your monthly expenses, you should pull up a monthly budgeting form at www.JOESANGL.com and do the following.

1. **Fixed Expenses**   Enter all of your fixed expenses - house payment, utilities, gasoline, car payments, credit card payments, groceries, cell phone, childcare, etc.   This also includes SAVING for retirement!
2. **Variable Expenses**   Enter the monthly average of all of your variable expenses - clothing, spending money, entertainment, dining out, etc.
3. **Known, Upcoming Non-monthly Expenses**   This is a KEY STEP!!!   If you do not add in all of those known, non-monthly upcoming expenses (like annual taxes, quarterly insurance premiums, vacation, and Christmas), you will continue to live the feast/famine lifestyle (more likely the famine lifestyle!!!!).   These types of expenses are BUDGET-BUSTERS.   Here is what I do.   I list all of the known, upcoming non-monthly expenses and place their annual cost next to them.   I then divide that number by twelve to determine how much I need to save per month.

Example of Known, Upcoming Non-monthly Expenses

	Annual Expense	Monthly Expense
Christmas	1,000	83
Health Club	780	65
Life Insurance	780	65
Auto Insurance	1,080	90
Vacation	2,160	180
Total	5,800	483

4. You now have a monthly budget that will change very little through the year!

So in this example, I would include a line item of $483 in my monthly budget for Known, Upcoming Non-monthly Expenses. This allows me to bring a stop to the feast, famine lifestyle!!!

Now, of course, the trick is to have enough cash on hand every month to make this monthly budget work!

Step 3: Save up at least three months worth of expenses.
WHAT?!!!! I am sure that is what many of you are saying right now! Yes, I did say that you need to save up at least three months of expenses. Remember in step two that you calculated your monthly expenses? Multiply that number by three, and you have your savings target. I call this savings the "Known Slumps Fund"! You **know** that slumps are coming, so be prepared!!! This is HUGE in eliminating that horrible feast/famine lifestyle!

You might be asking, "WHY?!!!. Why on earth should I save up at least three months worth of expenses?" I am so glad you asked that question!

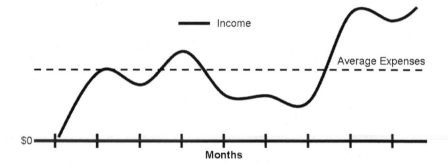

Let's say that you have monthly expenses of $3,000. This means that you need to have at least $9,000 in your Known Slumps Fund.

Let's look at a year's worth of expenses.

Month	Income
January	0
February	3,250
March	2,750
April	4,000
May	1,000
June	1,000
July	250
August	7,500
September	7,000
October	7,500
November	1,000
December	1,250
TOTAL	36,500

Now, it is easily seen that this person has earned enough to make it this year. They have taken in $36,500 for the year, BUT look at how irregular the income is! Have you seen something like that before in your business? This causes life to be CRAZY. In January, you are eating ramen noodles like they are going out of style. February through April are decent, but then it dies again May through July. Famine of the worst degree! All of the sudden, August through October are awesome! Feasts abound! Then November and December come in with back to back terrible incomes. Back to the ramen noodles!

What should you do? Get a Known Slumps Fund that equals three times your monthly expenses!

Let's see what difference that makes!

Month	Income	Outgo	Gain (LOSS)	Known Slumps Fund
January	0	3,000	(3,000)	6,000
February	3,250	3,000	250	6,250
March	2,750	3,000	(250)	6,000
April	4,000	3,000	1,000	7,000
May	1,000	3,000	(2,000)	5,000
June	1,000	3,000	(2,000)	3,000
July	250	3,000	(2,750)	250
August	7,500	3,000	2,500	4,750
September	7,000	3,000	4,000	8,750
October	7,500	3,000	4,500	13,250
November	1,000	3,000	(2,000)	11,250
December	1,250	3,000	(1,750)	9,500
TOTAL	36,500	36,000		

When you look at this chart you realize the POWER of having three months expenses in the bank! Whether you have a $500 income month or a $6,500 income month, you live on $3,000 that month. That means that you get to EAT!!! That means that you can save money (remember the monthly expenses includes retirement savings!). That means that you can have some fun each month!

The Known Slumps Fund will absorb the irregularities of your income! Fill up your Known Slumps Fund. It will take so much stress out of your life!!!

Step 4: Become personally debt-free.
What happens to your monthly expense load when you have no debt payments? It goes down. Way down! For a large majority of Americans, debt payments are at least 10% of the expenses. If you include the house payment, these debt payments are 35% or more of the monthly expenses! Imagine what your life looks like without ANY debt!

Isn't this EZ™?

How to Budget with Seasonal Income – Final Notes
Let's review the steps for budgeting with irregular income again.
Step 1: Recognize it!
Step 2: Determine your monthly expenses.
Step 3: Save up at least three months worth of expenses.
Step 4: Become personally debt-free.

Psst – I believe in you!

8 Budgeting Tips

Budgeting Tips

I have helped hundreds of people develop their budgets, and I wanted to include some tips that I have found to be very useful in the process of developing a hugely successful INCOME – OUTGO = EXACTLY ZERO™ budget.

Give

Did you notice that Ron and Judy's budget had $350 for giving? There is something incredible that happens when you gain control of your finances! You start having choices about where your money goes. It does not all have to go to pay the credit card payment, the car payment, the furniture payment, the student loan, and other debts.

As you become debt-free you *free* up money! This provides you with choices! I love choices! Everyone loves choices!

Ron and Judy love their home church. They have decided to tithe 10% of their gross income to their church which is $350. It is a cause they believe in deeply, and are pumped up to be able to support it.

What cause do you passionately believe in? Would that organization or individual benefit from financial support? Are you able to support it like you want to? A written budget will allow you to make this choice more easily!

Save

Did you also notice that Ron and Judy are saving $200 into an emergency fund? Ron and Judy have discovered that unexpected expenses sometimes crop up *during* the month. Unexpected expenses like a tire going flat on their car. It is not "Oh, honey, that couch is beautiful. Let's buy it!" It is not, "I want to go to the movies even though it is not in the budget."

When an unexpected expense crops up that is truly an "emergency", they will have the money available to cover the expense without it blowing up the budget or having to turn to debt!!! What an amazing thing!!! They have a plan for emergencies!!!

It is important to give every dollar a name.
Did you notice that EVERY dollar and cent has a name! Did it seem ridiculous to do this? Did it seem abnormal? It should! As my hero Dave Ramsey says, "Normal in America is B-R-O-K-E."

Now, I am not saying that you should list every single purchase you are going to make. I really do not care that your toothbrush will cost $2.43! Put the expenses into reasonable groups. I recommend that if a spending category is less than $10, it should probably be included together with some other group.

As an example, for Jenn and I, our "Grocery" fund includes everything we buy at Wal-Mart. This includes shampoo, toothpaste, toothbrushes, greeting cards, etc.

Give every dollar a name and spend it as planned. You will start to win financially!

Did you notice that Ron and Judy worked on their budget TOGETHER?
My marriage became unbelievably better when we started budgeting together! Why? We had to discuss our spending. We had to TALK! This required some "for better or worse" discussions! You know what? We had to go through some "for

worse" discussions so that now we can have the "for better" discussions! We had to agree on how we were going to spend our money.

We have had to discuss when the nephews and nieces have their birthdays, graduations, and weddings. Why? Because we send a gift to each one of them. It costs money. The benefit? I actually know when they are having their special day!!! I used to be the guy who was thanked by their nephews/nieces and said, "You're welcome!" I would immediately turn to Jenn and ask, "What did we send them and why?" Now, I really know!

We have had to make HARD decisions – HARD DECISIONS – like what we were going to cut out of the budget in order to pay cash for surgeries that were very costly and unplanned. We could have tapped into our emergency fund for those surgeries, but we knew that we had four months until the bills would get through the insurance companies and that if we worked together, we could pay cash for them. Did you know that by paying cash within 30 days of receiving the final bill, we were given a 10% discount? We did not even have to ask for it!!! It was written on the bill! I just saved someone $500 with this one line of information!

Jenn and I also make decisions on how much we are going to spend on vacations, gifts, how much to contribute to retirement, how much extra to pay on the house, and how much we are going to give. These are AWESOME discussions that enable us to better understand each other and help us work on our future plans TOGETHER!

Cash Envelopes
Studies repeatedly show that you will spend less if you pay with cash. When you pay with cash you really get the feeling that you are spending real money.

Pull out your credit card and place a $100 bill next to it. Which one is your eye drawn to? Which would you rather have? Guess what? It's the same one that retailers want from you ! CASH!

Still don't believe me? Read on!

Compare McDonald's cash transactions versus their debit/credit card transactions. The average debit/credit card transaction amount is over 40% more than the average dollar amount of each cash transaction.

Burger King statistics show that overall, "Visa and MasterCard studies show that the average ticket size of ... purchases made with credit cards exceeds that of cash transactions—about 30% more according to Visa."[1]

I use a cash envelope for my spending money, groceries, dining out, entertainment, clothing, and household spending (stamps, mulch, etc.) fund.

Why? Because I don't have to keep track of how much I have spent in each category. All I want to know is how much I have left in each fund anyway! Think about it. Do I care if the grocery fund started out with $300? NO! All I care about is that it has $73 left for the rest of the month. If I have five days left before the month ends, then we are in great shape! If we have twenty days left, we are in trouble! In any case, I KNOW that I will never exceed the budgeted amount because we will not use the debit card or withdraw cash and violate the EZ Budget™!

Cash envelopes are one of the key reasons that Jenn and I are winning with our finances!

---

[1] www.digitaltransactions.net/files/acq.doc *Fast Food Cooks up a Winning Card Recipe* by Lauri Giesen

What if I don't know EXACTLY how much some of my bills will be?

There are many items that you may need to estimate for your budget. A few of them may include usage-based utilities like electricity, natural gas, water, sewer, etc. Others may need to be estimated because it is difficult or impossible to know the number exactly. This would include items like groceries and gasoline.

What should you do? Estimate the cost. You can probably get within $10 of the actual cost.

If it is an item that you will use on-line bill payment or a written check to pay, then it could become a problem if you do not keep track of your checking account balance. One thing that helps this to NEVER become a problem for Jenn and I is we maintain a cushion in the checking account of $200 - $300. Because of this cushion I do not have to track my balance every single day. This does NOT give Jenn or me a license to spend more than we have budgeted. If an item comes in higher than budgeted, the budget is adjusted to make it EZ™!

In Ron and Judy's budget, they have budgeted an estimate for their groceries of $300. Now, the power happens right here. If they would have budgeted $350, I would bet that they would have spent exactly $350! HOWEVER, because they budgeted $300, they will now spend EXACTLY $300! There is power in a having a plan!

What do I do if I have an unexpected emergency?

Review it with you spouse. Identify what an emergency is. Inevitably, you will have an unexpected financial emergency occur. Right now, what would be a financial emergency for you? Would it be the transmission going out on your car? What about the tires needing replaced? How about a great price on a new couch? What if it is Christmas? What about a newfound health issue?

The bottom line is that you will have financial emergencies happen.

I must first address what a true financial emergency is. I would argue that replacing car tires should not be an emergency! Tires wear out! You drove the car, the rubber wore off, and now they need replaced. This should NOT be an emergency. I would argue that Christmas is not an emergency. It is always on December 25th. Every year you have twelve entire months to prepare for it!

The fact is that I cannot dictate what qualifies as an emergency for you. You will! Your homework assignment is for you and your spouse to sit down and determine what is truly a financial emergency. These emergencies are what you will use your emergency fund for! WRITE THEM DOWN! That way, when the emergency arises, you will have already discussed it with your spouse ahead of time and you will not feel guilty about utilizing the emergency fund for it.

We, the undersigned, hereby agree that the below events are classified as "EMERGENCIES". Emergency Fund money can be used to pay for these events.

_____   _____
        Signature 1   **Signature 2**

How do I budget for non-monthly expenses?
Whenever anyone starts to force their money to behave, they experience "budget-busting" expenses. Many times these are non-monthly expenses. Items like auto insurance, property taxes, homeowner's insurance, vacations, Christmas, and life insurance annual payments can blow up the budget.

Should any of these expenses be a surprise? NO! If we stop and think about it, these are *known* expenses. Yet somehow we allow them to become "Budget Busting" expenses. I have lived without budgeting for these types of expenses. It REALLY makes money management difficult!

So what should you do? Plan.

Let's say the following are your known, upcoming non-monthly expenses.

	Annual Expense	Monthly Expense
Christmas	1,000	83
Health Club	780	65
Life Insurance	780	65
Auto Insurance	1,080	90
Vacation	2,160	180
Total	5,800	483

Example of Known, Upcoming Non-monthly Expenses

If you include a line item for "Known, Upcoming Non-monthly Expenses in your budget for $483 each month, you will never again have your budget blown up by these expenses!

When budget-busting expenses do show up, do not give up! You are starting to make your money behave! You need to EXPECT these budget-busting expenses to impact you in your first few budgets.

What if I get paid weekly or bi-weekly and can't do just a monthly budget?
Budget using a weekly budget that is for the entire month. See the chapter on weekly budgeting.

What if I have a highly seasonal income, can I budget?
Many have used this as an excuse to not create a budget! Lousy excuse!!! People using this excuse will continue to lose financially until they force their money to behave. See the chapter on seasonal budgeting.

Give yourself a raise – Figure out how to save money in your budget.
How much money do you need to earn to bring home $100 extra dollars? The answer is: approximately $150. Why? Because Uncle Sam takes his share! For the average family, 1/3 of the pay is taxes and you will be able to bring home about 2/3 of the pay. Two-thirds of $150 is $100.

Now, here is another question. How much money do you need to save in your budget to free up $100 to spend on something else or to save? The answer is: $100!!! There are no more taxes! You have already brought home the money. It has already been taxed. $100 = $100.

Think of it like this. If you manage to spend $300 less per month on your monthly budget, it is the same as receiving a $450/month raise!!!

Very cool.

This becomes easier as you go along.
The first month may be tough. The second month is a little easier. The third month is even easier. After a complete year of monthly budgeting, you will have absorbed the entire blast of "budget-busting" costs!

After one year of forcing your money to behave, you will have experienced AMAZING HOPE-INSPIRING changes in your marriage, in your personal life, and in your finances! HOPE will be restored! You will have a plan! You will be managing your money instead of the money managing you!!!

I just cannot write in words the LIFE-CHANGING impact that this can have on your marriage and life! Jenn and I will never be the same.

Never **EVER** be the same.

Having an emergency fund is important.
My great-aunt, Aunt La, always said it was nice to have a little jingle in your pocket. What she was really saying was that it is nice to have some extra money available to you so that when you need it, it will be there!

If you do not have a cash emergency fund, you will always be at risk of turning to debt when financial emergencies arise.

If Ron and Judy have no savings, then anything could become a financial emergency. They could have a flat tire and need to replace it. Where will the money come from? If they have $0 sitting in savings, they may be highly tempted to turn to debt to pay for it.

If they had $1000 sitting in their emergency fund, they could have decided together that it qualifies as an emergency and therefore avoid debt.

The emergency fund is what will give you breathing room. It will remove stress.

Think about this next question for at least ten seconds:

Question: How would it feel to have $1,000 just sitting in your savings account?

Wow! I still get the same feeling of relief that I had when I first got there! It is an unbelievable feeling!!! It is a freeing feeling!!! Do you agree?

Think about this next question for 10 seconds:

Question: How would it feel to have $10,000 just sitting in your savings account?

Unbelievable!!! This is so liberating! When you get into this financial condition, you can be freed up spiritually! You are no longer consumed with the "how on earth am I going to get ahead?" question. You are able to focus on what you were put on this earth to do!!!

Guess what? You can have $10,000 just sitting in your savings account!

Avoid "The FEVER" – Listen to your spouse!
As I shared at the beginning of this book, I really wanted the new Honda Odyssey when it first came out! It was in the early days of DVDs and this van could actually be purchased equipped with a DVD player integrated into its sound system! Woo Hoo!

We had recently welcomed our first child into the family, and Jenn and I had made a deal that when we had child number two we would purchase a mini-van. Since we were planning on child number two showing up a couple of years after our firstborn, I started looking into mini-vans.

I caught a horrible case of car fever. I began to work the numbers in our "budget".

The budget did not meet the INCOME – OUTGO = EXACTLY ZERO™ principle! ☺

I had a HUGE car payment plugged into the budget, and I was not even focused on eliminating this HUGE issue. The shortage in the annual budget was over $10,000, and I was focused on reducing small costs like cable TV and other items that do not even remotely come close to making the budget equal zero.

This budget was upside down by thousands of dollars, and I still wanted to do it! How would I have managed to make up the difference? Debt!

All I can say is "Thank God for an awesome, discerning wife!" Jenn took one look at the budget and said, "Cut out the car payment!" When I did that, the budget had a chance of becoming EZ™.

What am I trying to say here? I am telling you that there will be times that you "get the fever" to purchase something. It may be a car. It may be a house. It may be land. It may be something else. All I am saying is that when you put it on paper and work with your spouse or accountability partner, the chance of you making a poor financial decision is greatly reduced!

Budget every single month.
Every single month is different. One month is full of weddings. Another is full of Christmas. Summer is full of travel while Fall is full of school tuition, clothes and books. Every single month is different! Take the twenty minutes necessary to look at the calendar for the next 30 days and plan your spending on paper BEFORE the month begins.

Why monthly instead of weekly, quarterly or annually? Most of your ongoing expenses will happen monthly, and it is usually the most appropriate timeframe for financial planning.

Jenn and I were BROKE until we began to budget monthly. I had attempted budgets prior to December 2002. Notice that I said, "I". Jenn was not involved in the finances by MY choice, not her choice. The budgets that I had attempted were always on an annual basis and never broken down into monthly chunks. As a result, I had a budget that was not practical month after month.

Jenn and I had less than $1,000 in our savings account until we began to budget monthly. In fact, we averaged more like $4.13! We spent every dime we had plus we utilized our credit cards to live beyond our means. As a result, we not only had a very small savings cushion, but we were digging a deeper hole in debt!

We finally learned the first rule of holes ➔ When you are in one, stop digging!

By spending every single dollar on paper BEFORE we received the money and forcing our budget to be EZ^{TM}, we began to win with our finances.

Hold to the budget!
This seems obvious, but MAN it is hard to do this! Here is what happens. You will put together your first budget and water will drip from your ceiling onto the paper you printed your budget on!

"Are you committed to doing this?" the water drops will seem to ask. If you are not committed 100%, you will find a reason to say that the budgeting process does not work!

You must follow the budget! What do you do if you need to repair a leak in the roof or replace a flat tire? Find a way to do it without incurring debt. You can do this. I know of many stories where people's commitments are tested, and they pass with flying colors!

Flat tire? A $10 used tire gets them around until they can afford a new one.

Engine dies on the car? Carpooling gets them to and from work until they can afford to fix it! As I write this book, I know of a person who lives in the country, but rides a bike to work to save money.

Sound crazy? Sound abnormal? It is! Guess what? I am not broke anymore! I decided once and for all that debt was not helping me, and that interest needed to work FOR me instead of AGAINST me.

Follow your EZ Budget™. Make it EZ™. You will NEVER regret it!

Say "NO!" to yourself the 1st, 2nd, 5th, 82nd and 512th times that you are tempted to break the budget.
This is just like dieting. It is easy to tell yourself "NO!" the first and second times you are tempted, but what about the 56th time? What about the 125th time? Preparing and living by an EZ Budget™ is what will allow you to say NO!!! and win with your finances!

If you happen to fall off of the wagon, pull out the wagon stapler and staple yourself back to the wagon!

Teach your children this stuff!

I love public education. We have the best schools in the world, but they do not do the best job of teaching children how to handle their finances.

Schools will not teach your children how to manage money.

I went through twenty years of formal education, and I learned a lot about how to make money. I learned very little about what to do with that money once I earned it!

Can you imagine where your children will be if they learn this at age six? They can understand INCOME – OUTGO = EXACTLY ZERO™ by age six. Trust me on this! Teach your children, and you will leave a legacy!

Psst – I believe in you!

9 Savings

Saving money is crucial.

In the hundreds of counseling sessions that I have held, I am still amazed at how little money people have saved! It does not matter how much folks are earning, they still manage to spend it all PLUS more!

$20,000/year income – No savings!
$50,000/year income – No savings!
$100,000/year income – No savings!
$200,000/year income – No savings!

It is crazy! In surveys of my financial classes, it is shocking to see that my seven-year-old daughter has more money saved than 70% of those in attendance.

Not shocking to you?

Perhaps it becomes so when I reveal to you that my daughter has $140 in her savings account.

More than 70% have less than $114 in their savings account! It makes me CRY! It makes me ANGRY! It makes me say, "WHAT IS GOING ON? WHY ARE WE ALLOWING OURSELVES TO GET CAUGHT IN THIS HORRIBLE TRAP?"

It made me leave corporate America and start a crusade to help others win with their finances!

Chapter 9 – Savings

Folks, we simply MUST save money!

As Jenn and I have gone through years of budgeting and working toward financial freedom, we have discovered that there are three key reasons you need to save money.

Three Reasons To Save Money
1. Unknown, Unexpected Emergencies
2. Known, Upcoming Expenses
3. Funding your Dreams

Unknown, Unexpected Emergencies
Life is going to happen! Someone will get sick. The car will break down. The appliance will fail. Something in the house will quit working. Unexpected bills will show up. Emergencies are going to happen!

If you do not have at least $1,000 sitting in an emergency buffer fund, you are at risk of acquiring debt! What will you do if the car breaks down? Turn to debt! What will you do if the kids have to go to the doctor? Turn to debt! This does not need to be the case!

Let's think about this. Is it surprising that cars break down? Is it surprising that children will need new clothes? Is it surprising that Christmas is in December this year? Is it surprising that you will have doctor bills sometime in the future?

Yet, many times we act as if it is a total surprise! Why? Because there was no plan and there was nothing saved for this so-called "emergency." Why was it an emergency? Because there was no money saved up!

I learned that in order to win with finances, I have to call things what they really are instead of what I hope or want them to be. Children growing, cars breaking down, roofs needing replaced, and medical bills are all going to happen! We do not know which car, which roof, or which illness will occur, but we *do* know that it will happen. Let's save for them!

To do this, you need to save at least $1,000 in an emergency buffer fund! The more the better! If you own a home or have children, it is even better to have at least $2,500 in case the furnace goes out or a child gets sick!

I regularly see an example in nature that really demonstrates the need for a buffer. I live in South Carolina, and we have large man-made lakes that were built by the Army Corps of Engineers to collect water for use during droughts and to generate electrical power.

These lakes have no protection along their shores. When crazy people (like me) go to the lake and ski, we send large waves crashing to shore.

The man-made lake has no protection. It is exposed. The first wave that comes in will smash with full-strength into the shore resulting in severe erosion. It is visible. It is tangible.

On the other hand, I have been to Minnesota many times for vacation. It is a state known as "The Land of 10,000 Lakes" – all of its lakes are natural lakes.

I also ski up and down these lakes and send large waves crashing to shore. BUT, it is different for these natural lakes. When a wave rolls in, lily pads start to weaken the wave. After encountering the lily pads, the wave encounters the bulrushes which weaken the wave further. The result? The shoreline is greatly protected against erosion!

LESSON: *Natural lakes have natural built-in protection!*

What about police officers? They all wear bulletproof vests. Why?

On Sundays, we have police officers at our church. They all have bulletproof vests on. Do they really believe they are in danger of being shot on Sunday at church?

They wear bulletproof vests because they know that they might get shot at one day. So my question is this: The bulletproof vest is so hot and uncomfortable, why don't they just wear the bulletproof vest on the day they are going to get shot?

Sounds silly doesn't it? Everyone knows you cannot predict the day when someone will shoot at you!

LESSON: *Police officers wear the vest EVERY SINGLE DAY!*

As I write this, I have received word that a member of our church who is a police officer was investigating a robbery in progress. He was shot at least four times. His arm took two shots and his VEST took another two. I am glad he was wearing the vest! And so is he!

For my manufacturing friends, here is another example.

I have had this customer that orders crazily. They order 50,000 parts at one time. Now, I know that they cannot possibly use 50,000 parts in the next six months, but they are ordering the parts today and are demanding their delivery by tomorrow (Can you say automotive industry?). By the way, this customer has the ability to make these demands, and my future business depends on my ability to meet these short-notice orders.

It will take at least two weeks for me to produce 50,000 parts. What do you think I do? I keep more than 50,000 parts on the shelf. Why? Because I cannot afford to let my "crazy" customer mess up my manufacturing floor with their order pattern. As a result, my emergency buffer fund of 75,000 parts will absorb their order, and I will be able to run the shop in the most economic way without even being affected by this "strange" order.

Why was I able to do this? Because I had a plan, prepared appropriately and had inventory on hand.

LESSON: *Businesses carry inventory to protect themselves!*

So IF you know that:
• Natural lakes have natural barriers
• Police officers wear bulletproof vests, and
• Businesses carry inventory

Why on Earth would you operate your finances without the protection of an emergency fund?

If you do not have the protection of savings, every single wave that life sends at you (or crazy customer order) will erode your ability to win financially. It will cause you to change the way you manage money every single time any little thing happens. This is what I call "letting your money manage you."

If you have an emergency buffer fund, you will be able to continue on with life even during a financial emergency. If an "emergency" happens, you are prepared. You had a plan. You can just pay for it. This is what I call "managing your money."

If you do not have an emergency buffer fund, every problem you have will be accompanied by a money problem. Car problem? Money problem, too. Washing machine breaks? Money problem, too. By establishing an emergency buffer fund, you will just have a car problem or washing machine problem. The money part is taken care of!

One additional note to husbands. By establishing an emergency buffer fund, you will be enabling your wife to live a lower-stress life! She needs to know that there is money there to absorb life's waves!

Jenn has required us to have an extra-large emergency buffer fund. IT IS SO WORTH IT!

Known, Upcoming Expenses
When Jenn and I first started budgeting, we had another word for known, upcoming expenses. BUDGET-BUSTER! These expenses blew up the budget because they seemed to appear at the last minute, and we had not saved up money for the expense.

After experiencing a month with a huge budget-busting expense, I felt like the snake that swallowed an antelope! I would walk around rather stunned saying, "I can't believe I ate that whole expense this month. I sure am hungry!!!"

Here is a list of common known, upcoming (budget-busting) expenses:
- Real Estate Property Taxes – Semi-annual payments
- Life Insurance – Annual premium
- Auto Insurance – Quarterly or annual premiums
- Health Club – Annual fee
- Golf Club – Annual dues
- Professional Organization – Annual dues
- Vacations – Whenever
- Income Taxes – Quarterly estimated or annual payments
- Christmas – Annually (in December ☺)

The list could go literally go on and on. But the point is that these items are really KNOWN, UPCOMING expenses aren't they? The property taxes should not be a surprise! No matter how much Christmas season creeps up on folks, it really shouldn't be a surprise. Should it?

Saving for these types of expenses is NOT difficult!

How much will you be spending on Christmas this next year? $1,000? OK. If you are budgeting in January, then you need to save $83.33 this month and every month for the rest of the year. In December, you will have $1,000 available for Christmas!

Christmas Example:

$1,000	/	12	=	$83.33
Expense		Months Left		$/month to save

Got it? This may make some of your monthly budgets tighter, but remember how hard it is to handle a "Budget Buster" expense all in one month! You will be sufficiently motivated to save *every* month!

Expense	Cost		Months		$/Month
Vacation	1,200	/	12	=	100
Income Taxes – Est. Qtrly	1,200	/	3	=	400
Health Club	720	/	12	=	60
Property Taxes - Semiannual	600	/	6	=	100
			Total Per Month		660

Another way to look at this is to understand the escrow account for your house payment. For those who have an escrow account, there is never a concern about being able to pay for the property taxes or homeowner's insurance. Why? The mortgage company takes the annual cost of the taxes and insurance and divides it by twelve – then collects that amount every single month.

Create an "escrow" account for your known, upcoming, non-monthly expenses. I do this, and it has made budgeting for these larger known, upcoming expenses SO easy to manage!

Use the worksheet on the next page to determine how much you need to save each month to fund your "escrow account for KNOWN, UPCOMING EXPENSES".

KNOWN, UPCOMING EXPENSES

Expense	Cost		Months		$/Month
		/		=	
		/		=	
		/		=	
		/		=	
		/		=	
		/		=	
		/		=	
		/		=	
		/		=	
		/		=	
		/		=	
		/		=	
			Total Per Month		

Funding your Dreams
This is the WHOLE REASON that Jenn and I strive to manage our money well! We have dreams that we want to accomplish!

We all have dreams! What dreams did you write down earlier? How much will it cost to fund those dreams?

I don't know about you, but I get no inherent joy out of paying my electrical bill on time. I know that I should pay it on time and that I do like electricity, but it just doesn't pump me up. What pumps me up is being able to realize a dream!

Jenn and I had the dream of moving back to Anderson, South Carolina to be a part of the church we had helped start up. We had the dream of starting a financial ministry there. To do so, we knew that it would require a major pay cut. After four years of focused funding of this dream, we were able to accomplish our dream and move back to Anderson – with a 50% pay cut – and we are still smiling about it! We have been able to fund a dream of ours!

I want you to be able to achieve your dreams! I want you to be able to do EXACTLY what God has put you on Earth to do! I know you can do it!

I also know that if someone continues to be mired in debt and does not save money, they are at a great risk of never accomplishing their dreams! Dreams take money!

What are your dreams? What are you doing to accomplish your dreams? Earlier in this book, you listed your dreams. Now, why not put a cost and date next to them and calculate how much you will need to accomplish them?

FUNDING MY DREAMS

DREAM	WHEN	COST
	TOTAL COST	

Did the Total Cost of your dreams scare you? That's OK!!! That is why they are called dreams! But I am here to tell you that you can accomplish your God-inspired and God-given dreams!

How? You may ask. By becoming Debt-Free and Investing.

Psst – I believe in you!

10 Debt Freedom

Debt – What should you do?

Get rid of it!!! The 8th wonder of the world, compound interest, will work against you every single day that you are paying interest to someone else!

Interest payments have the power to keep you financially broke! I have yet to hear a financially free person tell me that their car loans and credit cards were the reasons they became wealthy!

So what should you do?

The first thing you should do is write down every debt you have on a single sheet of paper. You will need to know the name of the debt, the balance owed, and the minimum monthly payment.

Let's assume that the following list of debts is owed by Tom and Mary.

	Balance Owed	Monthly Payment
Car Loan	$5,500	$378
Credit Card	$7,400	$125
Student Loan	$11,500	$135
Total Debt	$24,400	$638

Assuming that Tom and Mary have committed to acquire NO NEW DEBT, a quick way to calculate their debt freedom date is to pretend that this is just one big debt with one big monthly payment.

	Balance Owed	**Monthly Payment**
Total Debt	$24,400	$638

If you divide the balance owed, $24,400, by the overall monthly payment of $638, you will see that debt freedom will be achieved in 38.2 months. See how that works?

What if Tom and Mary found a way to save $200 every single month from their current OUTGO? They will be able to use this money to reduce debt! By applying the extra $200 toward debt, their monthly debt payments will be $838! This brings their debt freedom date closer by over 9 months with a new debt freedom date of 29.1 months!

Balance Owed/Monthly Payment = $24,400/$838 = 29.1 months!

You may say, "You did not figure in the interest rates."

I would say, "You're right!" But, I also did not include pay raises, bonuses, tax returns, improved budgeting, found money (selling things!), or the level of your personal intensity in attacking this debt.

The bottom line is this. The average person I counsel that uses this calculation AND becomes sold-out committed to becoming debt-free usually accomplishes debt freedom in 2/3 of the calculated time!

How do you get debt-free faster? Sell some of the debt items!

Tom and Mary actually have two cars, but only one of them still has a payment. Every month, they are sending $378 to the finance company for this car. The car is worth $6,000. They could actually sell the vehicle and pay off the loan. And $500 would remain after paying off the loan. They could save the next two month's payments ($378 x 2 = $756) and have $1,256 to go buy a clunker that will get from point A to point B.

If they continued to save those old car payments they could bank the $378 every single month. If Tom and Mary do that for the next 6 months, they will have $2,268! Then they could sell the clunker for $1,000, and put it with the $2,268 to buy a better clunker! A $3,000 car should last for quite a while. They can now save up the $378 for twelve months. That is $4,536!!!

If Tom and Mary were determined to become extremely strange (and not broke anymore!), they could opt out of owning two vehicles! Sure, it would cause some changes to their daily routine, but they want out of debt!!! By going down to one car, they would be able to eliminate their $378 payment, and SAVE the $500 in equity on the vehicle PLUS the $378 monthly payment PLUS the taxes, license plates, insurance, repairs, and maintenance. Their savings over one year would look like this:

Item	Amount
Car Equity ($6,000 sell price - $5,500 loan)	$500
Car Payments ($378 x 12 months)	$4,536
Car Insurance	$400
Car Taxes, License Plates	$100
Maintenance/Repairs	$400
TOTAL	$5,936

In ONE YEAR, Tom and Mary could have $5,936 saved because they made the decision to live differently!!!

By using this money to spend toward their debt freedom date, the debt picture would now look like this:

	Balance Owed	Monthly Payment
Car Loan	-	-
Credit Card	$7,400	$125
Student Loan	$11,500	$135
Freed up money from budget		$200
Freed up money from car payment		$378
Freed up money from maintaining the car		$33
Freed up money from car insurance		$33
Freed up money from car taxes/license plates		$8
Equity from the sell of the car	-$500	-
TOTAL	$18,400	$912

PLUS there is a one-time $500 cash payment toward debt that is from the equity in the car.

The debt freedom date now looks like this:

Balance Owed/Monthly Payment = $18,400/$912 = 20.2 months!

If Tom and Mary sell their car, they will be FREE of DEBT in 1 year and 8 months! They will then have $912 EVERY SINGLE MONTH coming in that no longer has to go back out to service debt!

How much do you have going out EVERY SINGLE MONTH to make payments on your debt? Wouldn't you rather be able to save, spend or give that money instead of sending it off to the finance company?

Pay an extra $838. Every $838 buys you one month!
As we learned, if Tom and Mary decide to keep the car, but they manage to spend $200 less every single budget, they will have $838 a month to attack their debt.

Balance Owed/Monthly Payment = $24,400/$838 = 29.1 months!

Tom and Mary may not be happy with 29.1 months. They want to become debt-free sooner. Awesome! Here's another way to get there. For every $838 extra they pay toward the principal owed on this debt, their debt freedom date will move up one month!

This is when it gets really fun! Let's say that Tom and Mary have a $2,000 tax refund this year. They could use $1,676 to move their debt freedom date two months closer!

Debt	Monthly PMT	Months
$24,400	$838	29.1
$24,400 - $1,676 = 22,724	$838	27.1

Jenn and I had so much fun with this! Every time we had some extra money, we looked at the potential of moving up our debt freedom date.

For example, we looked into how soon we would become debt-free if we stopped contributing to my 401(k). Our debt-freedom date would have moved from 14 months to 10 months. Achieving debt freedom four months sooner was not convincing enough for us to stop the retirement plan contributions, so we made the decision to continue funding the 401(k).

The key here is that we made a **decision**. It was our **choice**. We thought through it. We talked it over. We ran the numbers. In the end, in this case, it was not worth it.

It is incredibly empowering when you work together and make decisions for your money instead of your money making decisions for you!

The Debt Snowball
There are two general debt reduction strategies offered by financial counselors. One strategy is to focus on the highest

interest debt first. The other strategy is to focus on the smallest balance owed first. This strategy is called the Debt Snowball.

Jenn and I applied the Debt Snowball method. I recommend this method because you see individual debts disappearing from your payment schedules more quickly! When I was able to stop writing checks to Capital One, I realized that I really was making progress!

Let me explain the process for using the debt snowball.
1. List all debts from the smallest balance owed to the largest
2. Pay the minimum payment on all debts except for the smallest one
3. Pay as much as you can on the smallest debt!
4. When the smallest debt is paid, take the monthly payment you were making on that debt and add it to the monthly payment you were making on the second smallest debt.
5. Continue this process with a vengeance until you are DEBT FREE!!!

Debt Snowball Example

Debt Name	Balance	Monthly Payment
Doctor 2	320	50
Doctor 1	685	50
Hospital	1,300	50
Furniture	2,400	75
Car	5,000	140
Credit Card 1	6,000	160
Credit Card 2	7,500	115
TOTAL	23,205	640
Months Until Debt Freedom!	**36.3**	

A person has $23,205 in debt with $640 going out in monthly payments. The calculated Debt Freedom Date is 36.3 months.

After **6.4 Months** - Paid off "Doctor 2"!

Debt Name	Balance	Monthly Payment
Doctor 2	PAID	OFF!
Doctor 1	365	100
Hospital	980	50
Furniture	1,920	75
Car	4,104	140
Credit Card 1	4,976	160
Credit Card 2	6,764	115
TOTAL	19,109	640

The $50 payment that was going to "Doctor 2" is added to the "Doctor 1" payment.

Now "Doctor 1" will receive $100/month.

After **10.0 Months** - Paid off "Doctor 1"!

Debt Name	Balance	Monthly Payment
Doctor 2	PAID	OFF!
Doctor 1	PAID	OFF!
Hospital	798	150
Furniture	1,646	75
Car	3,593	140
Credit Card 1	4,392	160
Credit Card 2	6,344	115
TOTAL	16,773	640

The $100 payment that was going to "Doctor 1" is added to the "Hospital" payment.

Now "Hospital" will receive $150/month.

After **15.4 Months** - Paid off "Hospital"!

Debt Name	Balance	Monthly Payment
Doctor 2	PAID	OFF!
Doctor 1	PAID	OFF!
Hospital	PAID	OFF!
Furniture	1,248	225
Car	2,849	140
Credit Card 1	3,541	160
Credit Card 2	5,733	115
TOTAL	13,370	640

The $150 payment that was going to "Hospital" is added to the "Furniture" payment.

Now "Furniture" will receive $225/month.

After **20.9 Months** - Paid off "Furniture"!

Debt Name	Balance	Monthly Payment
Doctor 2	PAID	OFF!
Doctor 1	PAID	OFF!
Hospital	PAID	OFF!
Furniture	PAID	OFF!
Car	2,072	365
Credit Card 1	2,654	160
Credit Card 2	5,095	115
TOTAL	9,822	640

The $225 payment that was going to "Furniture" is added to the "Car" payment.

Now "Car" will receive $365/month.

After **26.6 Months** - Paid off "Car"!

Debt Name	Balance	Monthly Payment
Doctor 2	PAID	OFF!
Doctor 1	PAID	OFF!
Hospital	PAID	OFF!
Furniture	PAID	OFF!
Car	PAID	OFF!
Credit Card 1	1,746	525
Credit Card 2	4,442	115
TOTAL	6,188	640

The $365 payment that was going to "Car" is added to the "Credit Card 1" payment.

Now "Credit Card 1" will receive $525/month.

After **30.0 months** - Paid off "Credit Card 1"!

Debt Name	Balance	Monthly Payment
Doctor 2	PAID	OFF!
Doctor 1	PAID	OFF!
Hospital	PAID	OFF!
Furniture	PAID	OFF!
Car	PAID	OFF!
Credit Card 1	PAID	OFF!
Credit Card 2	4,060	640
TOTAL	6,188	640

The $525 payment that was going to "Credit Card 1" is added to the "Credit Card 2" payment.

Now "Credit Card 2" will receive $640/month.

After **36.3 months** - Paid off "Credit Card 2"!

Debt Name	Balance	Monthly Payment
Doctor 2	PAID	OFF!
Doctor 1	PAID	OFF!
Hospital	PAID	OFF!
Furniture	PAID	OFF!
Car	PAID	OFF!
Credit Card 1	PAID	OFF!
Credit Card 2	PAID	OFF!
TOTAL	0	640

DEBT FREEDOM!!!

Now "YOU" will receive $640/month!!!

AWESOME!!!!

You can complete your own Debt Freedom Date Calculation by visiting www.JOESANGL.com Click on "TOOLS".

Ben's Pickle Jar

I have this friend, Ben, who decided he was going to become debt-free. He is a single father raising his daughter. As he began to ponder ways to achieve debt freedom, he realized that he might have something of value that could really enable him to obtain debt freedom sooner!

Ben has this habit of buying crummy food items from the vending machines where he works. Egg salad sandwiches (maybe made from ostrich eggs?), ham sandwiches (wild boar), and miscellaneous unidentified items are all within the realm of possibility when he makes a purchase from the vending machine. Poor taste in food notwithstanding, Ben has this habit of buying the food with a $5 bill. Any returned change is put into his pocket. Later in the day and having survived his first visit to the vending machine, he is drawn back to make another purchase. He makes this second purchase with another $5 bill. The change is put into his pocket again.

At the end of the day, he throws the change into a jar at home.

One day in passing conversation he mentioned that he likes to count change while watching football games. I asked him how much change he had, and he responded with, "Do you know those big pickle jars?"

"Yes," I replied.

"Well, I have one of those full of dollar coins," Ben said.

I nearly fell out of my chair!!! Do you know how much money that is?!

Long story short, Ben carried coins into the bank for the next three days (assuring them that he had not stolen them from a vending machine) and became debt-free!

Now, you may not have a pickle jar full of one dollar coins, but I would bet that you have something you could sell that would help speed you toward debt freedom!

Look around. What is it? A bicycle? A piece of furniture? A TV? Movies? Art? A boat? A car? You have something. I know you do!

No more debt!
Remember, NONE of this will work if you continue to obtain debt! The calculation for debt freedom only works if you are no longer using debt!

I have had spoiled brats tell me that they shouldn't sell their cars that have debt equal to an entire year's salary because they do not want their wife to have to drive around in an unsafe car. GIVE ME A BREAK!

If you are saying this, you are a spoiled brat! The real reason you are OK with crushing your budget with a huge car payment is that you are a spoiled brat, and are OK with living up to your eyeballs in debt and putting your marriage at risk over stupid vehicles that drop in value like a rock!!!

No more debt. I am through with it.

Psst – I believe in you!

11 Investing & Compound Interest

Investing

COMPOUND INTEREST

$100/month for 39 years = $1,000,000!

$250/month for 31 years = $1,000,000!

$500/month for 26 years = $1,000,000!

$1,000/month for 20 years = $1,000,000!

Got your attention?

This is real! This is not made up!

Let me introduce you to the 8th wonder of the world, **Compound Interest**. It will change your life!

Here is how Compound Interest works.

Let's say that you start with $0 and make the commitment to invest $100 every single month by setting up an automatic draft from your bank account into your investment.

In this example, I am assuming that this investment will deliver an increase of 12% every year (1% per month). In the first month, you invest your first $100.

Year	Month	Principal	Interest	Savings	Final Value	Invested
1	1	0	0	100.00	100.00	100.00

In month 2, you have $100 invested for the entire month. If it increases in value 1% each month (12% per year), your investment will grow by $1.00 ($100 x 1% = $1). You will also have an additional $100 automatically drafted from your bank account into your investment. This will bring your investment's value to $201 ($100 from previous month + $1 increase in value + $100 investment this month).

Year	Month	Principal	Interest	Savings	Final Value	Invested
1	2	100.00	1.00	100.00	201.00	200.00

The third month is where the POWER of Compound Interest starts to appear – even if it is in a small way!

In the third month you have $201 invested for the entire month! The $1 in value you gained last month will now earn money for you also! So this month you will see your investment grow $2.01 ($201 x 1% = $2.01). The $1.00 that you earned last month also earned you $0.01 this month!

Year	Month	Principal	Interest	Savings	Final Value	Invested
1	3	201.00	2.01	100.00	303.01	300.00

You may wonder why I am celebrating a stupid penny?!!! I am celebrating because I KNOW what this will look like when you have $100,000 invested! If you continue to invest $100 each month and achieve 12% annual growth, you will have $100,000 invested 20 years and 2 months from now!

Year	Month	Principal	Interest	Savings	Final Value	Invested
20	2	100,015	1,000	100	101,115	24,200

Look at that! You have $100,015 invested for the entire month. You will have contributed $24,200 (241 months x $100/month = $24,200), BUT your account will have gained $75,915 in interest!

Remember, it was $1.00 in month three that gained $0.01. Now, the $75,915 interest earned will earn you $759.15 in value IN

ONE SINGLE MONTH ($75,915 x 1% = $759.15)! The $24,100 you have actually invested will gain you $241.00 ($24,100 x 1% = $241) this month making the total gain $1,000 for that one month!

Now, this has been math intensive, and you may be tempted to check out on me (or burn this book!) Do NOT do it! I beg you! I plead with you to continue reading. All you need to know is that you need to invest money and do it every single month! To eliminate the math, let me just show you what $100/month at 12% annual growth looks like in 5 year increments.

($100/month with 12% annual growth)

Time	Value		Time	Value
5 years	8,167		30 years	349,496
10 years	23,004		35 years	643,096
15 years	49,958		40 years	1,176,477
20 years	98,926		45 years	2,145,469
25 years	187,885		50 years	3,905,834

That is just with $100 per month! After 40 years, you will have invested $48,000 (480 months x $100/month = $48,000), but your account will have grown to $1,176,477! Of that amount, $1,128,477 is interest!

Behold the power of Compound Interest!

Compound Interest can work against you, too!
Any loan that you pay an interest payment on is an example of compound interest working against you. A huge example of this is a home mortgage.

Let's say you have a home mortgage for $100,000 and are paying on this 30-year fixed rate mortgage with a 6% interest rate. How much interest will you pay the bank for that $100,000 loan if you pay it off in exactly 30 years with identical monthly payments?

$115,838

That is not a typo! You will pay $115,838 in <u>interest</u> to the bank for a $100,000 loan! You will make total payments of $215,838 to the bank for a loan of $100,000.

That is EXPENSIVE!

It is the reason that a bank's name is usually on the nicest, biggest building in town! They have a goal. Their goal is to make your money become their money. Thirty-year mortgages are just one excellent tool that they use to accomplish that goal!

If you were to instead pay off that $100,000 mortgage with the 6% interest rate in 15 years, you would pay a total of $151,895 for the $100,000 loan. You will have cut down the interest paid by $63,943 PLUS you will be the outright owner of your home 15 years *sooner*!

Do you see how compound interest can work against you in a big-time way?

Any type of loan on which you pay interest is a situation where compound interest is working against you.

I would also include zero-percent financing on a new car as an example of where compound interest is working against you. Why? Because the new car will depreciate in value nearly 60% over the next four years! This is a depreciating asset. If you finance a new $25,000 vehicle at 0% interest for five years, you will end up with a $10,000 vehicle. Where did the other $15,000 go? Behold the power of Compound Interest!

Retirement – How much will you need?

This is a key question that many people never think about. How much will you need to retire? If you make $50,000 a year, are you expecting to also have $50,000 a year in retirement? More? Less?

Once you've decided how much money you want to have each year during retirement, a relatively simple calculation can get you a good approximation of the amount you will need in your retirement investments.

For the equation you will need to know two numbers – (1) the amount of money you want to have each year and (2) the rate at which your account will be growing.

$$\frac{\text{Amount For Each Year}}{\text{Annual Growth Rate of Investment}} = \text{Nest Egg Required}$$

For example, if you would like to continue making $50,000 a year and you expect to earn 8% each year on your account, you will need $625,000 at retirement.

$$\frac{\text{Amount For Each Year}}{\text{Annual Growth Rate of Investment}} = \frac{\$50,000}{8\%} = \$625,000$$

If you have $625,000 in your retirement account and it grows 8%, you will earn $50,000. This allows you to spend $50,000 and keep your retirement account at $625,000!

Now, there is this thing called inflation that reduces the value of your money each year. It is the reason that a 15¢ candy bar thirty years ago now costs 50¢ and is half the size that it used to be!

Inflation has averaged between 3% - 4% for several years. To keep up with 4% inflation, you will need to give your nest egg and annual spending a 4% cost of living raise each year. If you plan on spending $50,000/year and you expect to earn 8% on your account AND you want to give yourself a cost-of-living raise every year, you will need to use the following equation.

$$\frac{\text{Amount For Each Year}}{\text{Annual Growth Rate of Investment - Annual Inflation Rate}} = \frac{\$50,000}{8\% - 4\%} = \$1,250,000$$

If you have $1,250,000 in your retirement account and it grows 8%, you will have growth equal to $100,000. To give your account a cost-of-living raise each year you will need to keep 4% of each year's growth in the account. In the first year of this example the 4% amounts to $50,000. You will now have $1,300,000 to produce next year's spending money and cost-of-living raise!

So there are three items that determine how much you will need for retirement.

1. Amount Wanted For Each Year – The more you want, the more you will need in your investment!
2. Growth Rate of Investment – The higher the growth rate, the less you will need.
3. Annual Inflation Rate – The higher the inflation rate, the more you will need.

If you were to assume a 12% return on your investment and keep the inflation rate at 4% and the amount at $50,000/year, you would only need $625,000.

$$\frac{\text{Amount For Each Year}}{\text{Annual Growth Rate of Investment - Annual Inflation Rate}} = \frac{\$50,000}{12\% - 4\%} = \$625,000$$

How much will you need at retirement?

Assumes 12% Annual Growth Rate of Investment
Assumes 4% Annual Growth Rate of Inflation

Amount For Each Year	Nest Egg Required	Amount For Each Year	Nest Egg Required
20,000	250,000	90,000	1,125,000
25,000	312,500	95,000	1,187,500
30,000	375,000	100,000	1,250,000
35,000	437,500	105,000	1,312,500
40,000	500,000	110,000	1,375,000
45,000	562,500	115,000	1,437,500
50,000	625,000	120,000	1,500,000
55,000	687,500	125,000	1,562,500
60,000	750,000	130,000	1,625,000
65,000	812,500	135,000	1,687,500
70,000	875,000	140,000	1,750,000
75,000	937,500	145,000	1,812,500
80,000	1,000,000	150,000	1,875,000
85,000	1,062,500	155,000	1,937,500

If your number does not absolutely make you want to yell out loud (in pain or in excitement – depending on how much you've already saved), I do not know what will!

If you have $143 saved up and are 53 years old, it is high time to get crackin'! If you are 20 years old, you need to start right now!

How do you start investing for retirement?
A question asked very frequently is "How do I start?" This is a great question! Let me first review the options most people have available to them.

Self-Directed Retirement Plans at Work
The number one way that Americans invest today is through self-directed retirement plans. If you are an employee of a for-profit business, chances are that your company offers a 401(k) plan. This plan allows you to invest your money into a variety of investments, each with a different level of risk and reward. The key feature of a self-directed retirement plan such as the 401(k) is that you can take portions of your pay and move this money

into your retirement plan without it being taxed! This is huge! For example, you can start investing $100 a month into your 401(k) and your take-home pay will not reduce by $100! The government is allowing you to use the taxes you would owe them to invest into your retirement plan. You will pay taxes when you begin withdrawing the money at retirement, but you will be able to use the money you would have paid the government (in taxes) to earn interest all the way up to your retirement. The chart below will helps explain this.

Year	Month	Tax-Deferred Value ($100/mo)	Post-Tax Value ($70/mo)	Difference
5	60	8,167	5,717	2,450
10	120	23,004	16,103	6,901
15	180	49,958	34,971	14,987
20	240	98,926	69,248	29,678
25	300	187,885	131,519	56,365
30	360	349,496	244,647	104,849
35	420	643,096	450,167	192,929
40	480	1,176,477	823,534	352,943
45	540	2,145,469	1,501,829	643,641
50	600	3,905,834	2,734,084	1,171,750

At the end of 5 years, the difference is only $2,450. However, the point has been clearly made that it is VERY IMPORTANT to build up the base quickly as soon as possible. Look at the difference in year 20 - $29,678! Look at the difference in year 30 - $104,849! If you have 50 years in front of you, the difference is $1,171,750!!!

Take the offer from Uncle Sam! Use your company's self-directed retirement plan.

Now, there are many different names for self-directed retirement plans. The name differences are related to their place in the federal tax codes. If you work for a non-profit organization, chances are that you have a 403(b), Simple IRA, or a Thrift Savings Plan.

In addition to the fact that you have the opportunity to invest your money pre-tax, many employers will match at least a portion of your contributions! This is FREE MONEY! I have worked for an employer that matched $1 for $1 up to 8% of my pay! This was an unbelievable opportunity, and I was able to take full advantage of that! Another employer matched $1 for $1 up to 6% of my pay. Still another matched $1 for $1 up to 3% of my pay, and then $0.50 for each $1 for the next 2% of my pay. In other words, if I put at least 5% they would put in 4%. Another matched $1 for $1 up to 3% of my pay. In ALL cases, it was FREE MONEY!

Here is what is very alarming to me. At every company I have worked for, there were MANY people who were not taking advantage of this FREE MONEY! I had one question for those people – WHY?!!!

Weak, lame, pathetic reasons were provided such as,
- "I can't afford to contribute."
- "I am living paycheck-to-paycheck already."
- "Our investment opportunities suck."

So ... Let me get this straight ... You are not able to afford having the company give you FREE MONEY? Do these people want to wear the T-shirt that says, "I choose to be broke!"? I don't get it!

Here is how you get started.
1. RUN to your Benefits Department and ask how you can sign up for your company's retirement plan.
2. Start contributing something. At least contribute enough to obtain everything the company will match for you!
3. As quickly as possible, move your investment contribution to at least 10% of your gross income. Yes, I know that this is a lot of money. You will NEVER regret this decision! Persons who contribute at least 10% of their gross income to

their retirement savings plan are the ones who will retire. Those who contribute 15% of their gross income will retire well!

A verse in the Bible comes to mind …

Proverbs 13:11 – "… he who gathers money little by little makes it grow."

What if my company does not have a self-directed retirement plan?

There are still many options available to you. This book does not include an exhaustive list, but the following options are some common ones available.

Roth IRAs

A website totally dedicated to this type of IRA is located at www.rothira.com.

A Roth IRA is an IRA in which you invest money that has already been taxed. The money can be invested in the same variety of stocks, mutual funds, and other investments just like any other IRA, but the difference here is that it will grow TAX-FREE!!! In our example of compound interest, which category was larger? The amount invested or the interest gained? The interest gained was the HUGE portion! It is all TAX-FREE!

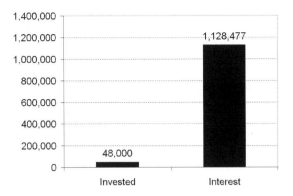

$100 invested monthly for 40 years @ 12% interest puts $1,176,477 in your pocket!

Traditional IRA
This is an IRA where you can invest before-tax money. The money can be invested in the same variety of stocks, mutual funds, and other investments just like any other IRA. Because you have the advantage of using before-tax money, you will be taxed when you start pulling money out at retirement.

You can start investing with as little as $25 as long as you sign up for automated monthly drafts of at least $25 from your bank account every month. Many different investment companies offer this option.

Real Estate
Your personal residence is another investment that grows tax-deferred and possibly tax-free! Although there are income limitations, you are currently able to earn $250,000 ($500,000 if married) TAX-FREE on the sale of your personal residence as long as you have lived in it as your primary residence for two of the past five years!

We have covered previously the need to pay off the house as soon as possible due to the fact that it is compound interest working against you. The beautiful thing with a house is that it is real tangible property that helps diversify your investment portfolio. It also has the intangible qualities of pride of ownership and security.

Automate. Automate. Automate.
Make your investments automatic. Arrange your investments so that the money is put into the account every single month. I have money auto-drafted from my account every single month for our Simple IRA (my crusade's self-directed retirement plan – similar to 401(k) and 403(b)), Roth IRA, and to our daughter's 529 college-savings plan. I do not have to think about it, BECAUSE it is automatic. It just happens. I never see the money! And every single month my net worth increases. WOW!

I was reminded of this again recently. When Jenn and I moved back to South Carolina, we changed to a new bank. This meant that the bank account that Melea's 529 college savings plan was auto-drafting from was now closed! Until I got the auto-draft set up to pull funds from my new bank, I had to write a check to the college fund. THAT was difficult! There are so many places I could have used that money! I believe that if I had to write a check every month to this savings account or to my investment accounts, there is a HIGH likelihood that my investing plan would be seriously off-track! MAKE IT AUTOMATIC!

Start NOW!
The sooner you start, the less you need to save each month to have enough for your goals! If you start at age 25 with $100 a month, invest for the entire 40 years to your retirement at age 65, and gain 12% you will have $1,176,477. If you wait until age 40 to start, you will have to invest $626/month to achieve the same wealth by age 65. If you wait until age 50 to start, you will have to invest $2,354/month!

Let's put this another way. Let's say that you are 25 years old and start investing $100/month right now and continue to invest for the next ten years. In ten years you stop contributing the $100/month. So, in this example, you have invested $12,000 by age 35. With 12% annual growth, your investment will be worth $826,986 upon retirement.

Now let's say that you have a friend named Bob who is also 25 years old, but he wants to put off investing for ten years. After ten years, he starts investing $100/month and does so for the next **thirty years**. In this example, Bob invested $36,000. That is $24,000 more than you. However, because Bob waited ten years, his investment is only worth $349,496 at retirement.

In fact, Bob will never catch up to you – because you started NOW!

Time	YOU	Bob
5 years	8,167	0
10 years	23,004	0
15 years	41,791	8,167
20 years	75,922	23,004
25 years	137,927	49,958
30 years	250,572	98,926
35 years	455,214	187,885
40 years	826,986	349,496
Total Invested	**12,000**	**36,000**

If you are investing, time is your friend. Start NOW!

Opportunity Cost

How much are you currently spending to service debt every single month?

For the average family in America, it is between $500 and $1000 PER month. What if you did not have to send that money to the banks every single month? What would you do with that money?

That is the definition of Opportunity Cost. You can only use your money once to purchase something. Once that money is spent, it is gone! When we encounter some extra money, Jenn and I stop and ask ourselves the question, "What are the different opportunities we have to use this money?"

For example, when Jenn and I were focused intensely on becoming debt-free, we looked at the possibility of stopping our contribution to the 401(k) so that we could use that money to become debt-free faster. However, when we looked at the big picture (knowing the power of compound interest, Proverbs 13:11, and other facts) we saw that this move would help us become debt-free only four months faster than if we kept contributing to the 401(k). Achieving debt-freedom four months sooner was simply not motivating enough for us to make this move.

The key here is that we looked at the different opportunities before spending the money. We chose the option that suited us best. The key words here are that we looked at our options BEFORE making a CHOICE. We CHOSE what we were going to do with our money.

That is so powerful! Instead of our money managing us, we were managing it! What a novel concept!!! I love this stuff because this is what is enabling Jenn and me to accomplish exactly what we have been put on this earth to do!

Investments go UP in value

When you are around me, please do not use the following sentence. "I invested in a new car for the family." Cat's claws on a chalkboard are less annoying than this statement!

Investments go UP in value. A new car will go WAY DOWN in value. It will depreciate around 60% in the first four years after its purchase! Yes, I know that it looks nice, but is it worth it? It may be for you, but it is unlikely to be worth it for me.

The goal is for your investments to go UP in value. Never forget this.

Summary of Investing

Why do you want to achieve financial freedom? Have you sat down with your spouse and wrote out a plan for your life yet? What exactly is it that you have been put on this earth to do? God created you for a very specific reason.

When you have a written plan for your life with specific hopes and dreams, it will drive you to manage your finances better. It is not going to just happen. It is not hocus pocus. It requires FOCUS pocus. Your attention to this is critical. Set up your investments, make them automatic, review them occasionally, and choose to win with your money!

Psst – I believe in you!

12 Insurance

Insurance. Ugh. I send so much money off to the insurance companies that at times I wonder if it is worth it. Ever wonder the same?

Here are all of the types of insurance that Jenn and I have:
- Term Life Insurance
- Homeowner's Insurance
- Auto Insurance
- Medical Insurance
- Long-Term Disability Insurance

I am going to explain why I carry these types of insurance. This is NOT the be-all end-all summary of all types of insurance. I am just explaining the types of insurance that Jenn and I own and WHY we own them.

My challenge to you is this. Can you explain the reasons you own your insurance to the same level of detail? I saved a ton of money when I started asking questions about my insurance and truly understood what I was purchasing.

Term Life Insurance
Jenn and I have 20-year level term life insurance. Level term means that the annual cost will remain the same for each of the next 20 years. If a policy costs $250 a year in the first year of the policy, then it will also cost me $250 a year every single one of the 20 years that this life insurance policy is in existence.

Term life insurance is very simple and very cheap. If we die at any time in that 20-year term, our beneficiaries will receive the full value of that life insurance policy. If the policy for me is $250,000 and I die sometime in the next 20 years, the policy will pay $250,000 to my wife.

It is VERY CHEAP and simple compared to any other insurance products out there. This is why we own this type of life insurance policy.

Why do I own a life insurance policy? To replace my income. I have around 10 times my annual income in term life insurance. If I die, I do not want Jenn to have to worry about replacing my income. Having term life insurance allows me to know that my income would be replaced.

Oh, and did I mention that it is VERY CHEAP? For a healthy non-tobacco using 30-year-old male, $500,000 coverage would cost around $21 a month. For a healthy, non-tobacco using 30-year old female, $500,000 coverage would cost around $20 a month. That's cheap for such great coverage.

A great web site to obtain term life insurance quotes from is www.zanderins.com

I know that there are other types of life insurance out there, but they are much more expensive when compared to term life insurance. Now, any type of life insurance is a bargain if you actually die and someone collects on it (feels wrong even writing this!). I like the cheapest method of protecting my family in the event of an untimely death, and I do that with term life insurance.

My goal is to become self-insured. If you are able to become and stay debt-free and invest wisely, you will have enough in the bank to not really need life insurance. Think about it. You die, but you leave behind $0 in bills and over $1,000,000 in the bank. You have probably become self-insured.

Life Insurance Tips
- Make sure you FULLY understand the product you are buying.
- Keep it simple.
- Get 8 – 10 times your annual income in term life insurance
- Pay annually – it is usually 10-30% cheaper!
- Obtain at least three quotes – at least one of these needs to be from an independent insurance agency
- Do not cancel an existing life insurance policy until you have a replacement life insurance policy in place! Do not allow a gap in coverage!
- Ask for a better deal – it is negotiable!
- Be careful purchasing insurance from a family member or a friend as your judgment could become clouded!

Homeowner's Insurance
You are required to acquire homeowner's insurance by the mortgage loan company. This is just smart! Homeowner's insurance costs between 0.5% and 1.0% of the home's value. For a $100,000 home, expect homeowner's insurance to cost from $500 - $1000 per year.

It is important to purchase guaranteed replacement value homeowner's insurance. If you buy insurance that is not guaranteed replacement value, you could end up still absorbing a major loss if the house were to be destroyed. For example, if you had homeowner's insurance that only paid $100,000 if your house were destroyed but your house has increased in value to $125,000, you could still lose $25,000. By having a guaranteed replacement value policy, you will ensure that your investment is fully protected.

If you do not own your home, but rent instead, you need to obtain renter's insurance. The owner of your residence does not carry insurance on your personal items that you own. You must carry the insurance for those items. It is called renter's insurance. Make sure you have this!

Homeowner's Insurance Tips
- ALWAYS have homeowner's insurance if you own a home – even if it is paid for!
- Make sure you FULLY understand the product you are buying.
- Get guaranteed replacement value insurance.
- Ensure that your home's contents are fully covered.
- If you have auto insurance or some other insurance, ask for the "bundle" discount. Most insurance companies offer a package discount if you hold more than one policy with that company. It can result in substantial savings!
- Consider increasing the deductible. If you are managing your money well and have 3 – 6 months worth of expenses in an emergency fund, you may consider increasing the deductible. This will result in a lower insurance premium.
  - Example: If you increase your deductible from $500 to $1,000 and the premium drops by $400 a year, this is probably a no-brainer. The premium is guaranteed to happen. An event requiring the use of the insurance is not guaranteed to happen. If you go 1.2 years without an event, you have made a wise financial decision. Even if an event happens 2 years down the road, you will pay the $500 more, but you will have saved $400 each year in premiums ($800).
- Shop around for the best rates every two years or so.
- Obtain at least one quote from an independent insurance agency.

Auto Insurance

The first reason Jenn and I have auto insurance is that it is required by law! That is a pretty motivating factor for us to get this insurance!

However, we do not have this insurance just because it is required by law. It allows us to transfer risk to the insurance company. If we had an automobile accident where we were at fault and our vehicle was destroyed, that would not be good. But we could just go buy another vehicle with the cash in our "new used car fund". Not fun, but we could do that easily.

But, what we could NOT do easily is pay for someone else's car that we also destroyed PLUS their medical bills which could easily add up to tens of thousands of dollars if not more than $100,000!

Therefore, Jenn and I carry auto insurance. We increased the deductible to $500 (up from $250) because the premium is around $200 a year less. If we go 1.25 years without causing an accident, we save money. See how that works?

	Lower Deductible ($250)		Higher Deductible ($500)	
Year	Known Cost	Deductible Cost	Known Cost	Deductible Cost
2007	Premium ($1,000)	$0	Premium ($800)	$0
2008	Premium ($1,000)	$0	Premium ($800)	$0
2009	Premium ($1,000)	$250	Premium ($800)	$500
TOTAL COST	$3,250		$2,900	

Because the savings of $200 is so good, I am willing to take the risk of having to pay a higher deductible. However, if the premium for going to a higher deductible ($250 to $500) only goes down by $20 a year, I am not going to take that deal. I would have to be accident-free for over 12 years to come out ahead financially. Statistics and my driving capability tell me that this probably will not happen!

Auto Insurance Tips

- ALWAYS have auto insurance
- Bundle with other types of insurance to get discounts
- Shop around every two years or so
- Obtain at least one quote from an independent insurance agency
- Obtain quotes with different deductibles
- Don't speed and DEFINITELY do not drive while under the influence of alcohol or drugs. You will be penalized SEVERELY in insurance costs – even to the point of becoming uninsurable. AND you put yourself and other's lives at risk. Don't do that!
- Be very cautious buying car insurance from family or friends without getting quotes from other places. Personal relationships could cost you big time on insurance premiums. Yes, I did just write that!

Medical Insurance

The cost of medical insurance is outrageous! It is out of control! It is HUGE! However, it MUST be a priority for you and your family! Why do you think that medical insurance costs so much? BECAUSE THE MEDICAL BILLS ARE SO HIGH!

Which would you rather have happen? Pay the HUGE medical insurance premiums or have one major illness/surgery and owe $20,000, $50,000, or even $100,000 without any insurance?

Jenn and I have medical insurance for the family. Everyone is covered. Yes, it is incredibly expensive. We will pay somewhere around $6,700 this year for our medical insurance!!! OUCH! And the insurance policy we carry will not pay until we have paid $3,000 in bills! What this means is that $9,700 has to leave our pockets PRIOR to any insurance kicking in.

This makes me want to CRY! It is horrible, BUT you must have insurance. I am shopping my insurance at this very moment to ensure I have the best deal available (I don't believe I do ...)

Jenn has had to have two major surgeries in the past 3 years. Each one cost over $14,000 each. The two surgeries occurred within 10 months of each other! Wow! If we would not have had medical insurance, we would have been in trouble!

Shop around. At least have insurance that covers the huge expenses – like a high deductible health insurance plan. This is a type of plan that requires you to pay a significant amount of medical expenses before the insurance will pay anything. After you hit the deductible, the plan will start paying the majority or all of the costs for the remainder of that year. This type of insurance is much cheaper than comprehensive care, but you should be financially OK if you have a fully-funded emergency fund of 3 – 6 months of expenses.

My medical insurance provider also negotiates rates with medical groups. As a result, I receive "discounts" on what the normal charge would be. I put quotes around discounts because it is hard to believe that a $1,000 charge per day for a hospital bed is a discounted rate. Argh!

Medical Insurance Tips
- Get over being irate at the cost and get covered – even a high deductible plan can seriously limit the costs you would pay in the event of a major medical event

- Shop around – usually whatever your employer offers you will be better than what you could get on the open market as an individual, but it is still worth it to shop around.
- Make sure you clearly understand what the insurance will and will not pay for!
- Make sure you CLEARLY understand what the insurance will and will not pay for!
- Make sure you CLEARLY UNDERSTAND what the insurance will and will not pay for!
- Yes, I wrote it 3 times! (It's important!) ☺
- Have insurance at all times. You don't know when you are going to need it.

Long-Term Disability Insurance (LTD)

If I get injured and I am unable to speak, write, or perform the duties of my crusade, I will no longer be able to produce an income. Yet I am still alive. How would I be able to generate an income to pay for my ongoing expenses? LTD insurance ensures this for me. It is provided by my employer (many employers provide this), and it is extremely cheap for employers to provide it for their employees (unless you sky-dive or participate in other high-risk activities).

Should I become disabled, LTD Insurance will pay 50 – 60% of my income, until I am able to perform my duties again.

I want same-skill LTD insurance. Why? Because I may recover and be able to walk again, but I may be unable to speak. Speaking is a large part of my crusade. As a result, I will not be able to do what I have been *made* to do. I want insurance that pays if I am unable to do what I have been *made* to do. I do not want insurance that will stop paying just because I am able to walk around again. In the insurance world, they call the type of insurance I want "Own Occupation". The type I do NOT want is "Any Occupation".

Long-Term Disability Insurance Tips
- Make sure you clearly understand the product you are buying.
- Obtain this insurance.
- Make certain you obtain "Own Occupation" LTD insurance.

Those are the types of insurance that Jenn and I own. Those are the reasons we own them.

Why do you own the policies you pay for?

Psst – I believe in you!

13 The Time Is Now!

So there it is. The exact steps that Jenn and I have taken to win with our money. How we moved far away from the days of $4.13 in the savings account.

We have been able to accomplish far more than what we ever thought possible – all because we said "NO!", "Wait!", and "Not now!" I have been able to embark on a crusade to take this knowledge to the nations.

The time has come. It is YOUR turn. I can not manage your money for you. I have poured myself into this book and its associated materials on www.JOESANGL.com so that you will be equipped to win financially.

It is time. Time to take your finances to the next level – to a place you only dreamed of achieving.

The world awaits you and your God-given dreams, talents, and abilities. Go become debt-free and pursue those passions with 100% abandon. I can't wait to hear what you get to be a part of and accomplish – all because one day you decided to win with your finances!

I have one favor to ask of you. Would you please carry this crusade to others? I need your help to take this to the nations! Give this book to a family member or friend. Help them put together their first-ever budget! The tools to get started are all available at www.JOESANGL.com

Contact Joe!

Joe is on a crusade to help others accomplish far more than they ever thought possible. As part of this crusade, Joe travels around the country to speak about finances and teach people the practical tools that will help others win financially!

To contact Joe about speaking or teaching at your organization, go to www.joesangl.com and click on "E-mail Joe" or e-mail him directly at josephsanglblog@yahoo.com!

Volume discounts are available for "I Was Broke. Now I'm Not!" by completing the contact form at www.joesangl.com or e-mailing josephsanglblog@yahoo.com